Table of Contents

Success Strategies

This section contains a list of test-taking strategies that you may find helpful as you work through the test. By taking what you know and applying logical thought, you can maximize your chances of answering any question correctly!

It is very important to realize that every question is different and every person is different: no single strategy will work on every question, and no single strategy will work for every person. That's why we've included all of them here, so you can try them out and determine which ones work best for different types of questions and which ones work best for you.

Question Strategies

Read Carefully

Read the question and answer choices carefully. Don't miss the question because you misread the terms. You have plenty of time to read each question thoroughly and make sure you understand what is being asked. Yet a happy medium must be attained, so don't waste too much time. You must read carefully, but efficiently.

Contextual Clues

Look for contextual clues. If the question includes a word you are not familiar with, look at the immediate context for some indication of what the word might mean. Contextual clues can often give you all the information you need to decipher the meaning of an unfamiliar word. Even if you can't determine the meaning, you may be able to narrow down the possibilities enough to make a solid guess at the answer to the question.

Prefixes

If you're having trouble with a word in the question or answer choices, try dissecting it. Take advantage of every clue that the word might include. Prefixes and suffixes can be a huge help. Usually they allow you to determine a basic meaning. Pre- means before, post- means after, pro - is

- 4 -

positive, de- is negative. From prefixes and suffixes, you can get an idea of the general meaning of the word and try to put it into context.

Hedge Words

Watch out for critical hedge words, such as *likely, may, can, sometimes, often, almost, mostly, usually, generally, rarely,* and *sometimes.* Question writers insert these hedge phrases to cover every possibility. Often an answer choice will be wrong simply because it leaves no room for exception. Be on guard for answer choices that have definitive words such as *exactly* and *always*.

Switchback Words

Stay alert for *switchbacks*. These are the words and phrases frequently used to alert you to shifts in thought. The most common switchback words are *but, although,* and *however*. Others include *nevertheless, on the other hand, even though, while, in spite of, despite, regardless of*. Switchback words are important to catch because they can change the direction of the question or an answer choice.

Face Value

When in doubt, use common sense. Accept the situation in the problem at face value. Don't read too much into it. These problems will not require you to make wild assumptions. If you have to go beyond creativity and warp time or space in order to have an answer choice fit the question, then you should move on and consider the other answer choices. These are normal problems rooted in reality. The applicable relationship or explanation may not be readily apparent, but it is there for you to figure out. Use your common sense to interpret anything that isn't clear.

Answer Choice Strategies

Answer Selection

The most thorough way to pick an answer choice is to identify and eliminate wrong answers until only one is left, then confirm it is the correct answer. Sometimes an answer choice may immediately seem right, but be careful. The test writers will usually put more than one reasonable answer choice on each question, so take a second to read all of them and make sure that the other choices are not equally obvious. As long as you have time left, it is better to read every answer choice than to pick the first one that looks right without checking the others.

Answer Choice Families

An answer choice family consists of two (in rare cases, three) answer choices that are very similar in construction and cannot all be true at the same time. If you see two answer choices that are direct opposites or parallels, one of them is usually the correct answer. For instance, if one answer choice says that quantity x increases and another either says that quantity x decreases (opposite) or says that quantity y increases (parallel), then those answer choices would fall into the same family. An answer choice that doesn't match the construction of the answer choice family is more likely to be incorrect. Most questions will not have answer choice families, but when they do appear, you should be prepared to recognize them.

Eliminate Answers

Eliminate answer choices as soon as you realize they are wrong, but make sure you consider all possibilities. If you are eliminating answer choices and realize that the last one you are left with is also wrong, don't panic. Start over and consider each choice again. There may be something you missed the first time that you will realize on the second pass.

Avoid Fact Traps

Don't be distracted by an answer choice that is factually true but doesn't answer the question. You are looking for the choice that answers the question. Stay focused on what the question is asking for so you don't accidentally pick an answer that is true but incorrect. Always go back to the question and make sure the answer choice you've selected actually answers the question and is not merely a true statement.

Extreme Statements

In general, you should avoid answers that put forth extreme actions as standard practice or proclaim controversial ideas as established fact. An answer choice that states the "process should be used in certain situations, if..." is much more likely to be correct than one that states the "process should be discontinued completely." The first is a calm rational statement and doesn't even make a definitive, uncompromising stance, using a hedge

- 6 -

word *if* to provide wiggle room, whereas the second choice is a radical idea and far more extreme.

Benchmark

As you read through the answer choices and you come across one that seems to answer the question well, mentally select that answer choice. This is not your final answer, but it's the one that will help you evaluate the other answer choices. The one that you selected is your benchmark or standard for judging each of the other answer choices. Every other answer choice must be compared to your benchmark. That choice is correct until proven otherwise by another answer choice beating it. If you find a better answer, then that one becomes your new benchmark. Once you've decided that no other choice answers the question as well as your benchmark, you have your final answer.

Predict the Answer

Before you even start looking at the answer choices, it is often best to try to predict the answer. When you come up with the answer on your own, it is easier to avoid distractions and traps because you will know exactly what to look for. The right answer choice is unlikely to be word-for-word what you came up with, but it should be a close match. Even if you are confident that you have the right answer, you should still take the time to read each option before moving on.

General Strategies

Tough Questions

If you are stumped on a problem or it appears too hard or too difficult, don't waste time. Move on! Remember though, if you can quickly check for obviously incorrect answer choices, your chances of guessing correctly are greatly improved. Before you completely give up, at least try to knock out a couple of possible answers. Eliminate what you can and then guess at the remaining answer choices before moving on.

Check Your Work

Since you will probably not know every term listed and the answer to every question, it is important that you get credit for the ones that you do know.

Don't miss any questions through careless mistakes. If at all possible, try to take a second to look back over your answer selection and make sure you've selected the correct answer choice and haven't made a costly careless mistake (such as marking an answer choice that you didn't mean to mark). This quick double check should more than pay for itself in caught mistakes for the time it costs.

Pace Yourself

It's easy to be overwhelmed when you're looking at a page full of questions; your mind is confused and full of random thoughts, and the clock is ticking down faster than you would like. Calm down and maintain the pace that you have set for yourself. Especially as you get down to the last few minutes of the test, don't let the small numbers on the clock make you panic. As long as you are on track by monitoring your pace, you are guaranteed to have time for each question.

Don't Rush

It is very easy to make errors when you are in a hurry. Maintaining a fast pace in answering questions is pointless if it makes you miss questions that you would have gotten right otherwise. Test writers like to include distracting information and wrong answers that seem right. Taking a little extra time to avoid careless mistakes can make all the difference in your test score. Find a pace that allows you to be confident in the answers that you select.

Keep Moving

Panicking will not help you pass the test, so do your best to stay calm and keep moving. Taking deep breaths and going through the answer elimination steps you practiced can help to break through a stress barrier and keep your pace.

Final Notes

The combination of a solid foundation of content knowledge and the confidence that comes from practicing your plan for applying that knowledge is the key to maximizing your performance on test day. As your foundation of content knowledge is built up and strengthened, you'll find that the strategies included in this chapter become more and more effective in helping you quickly sift through the distractions and traps of the test to isolate the correct answer.

Now it's time to move on to the test content chapters of this book, but be sure to keep your goal in mind. As you read, think about how you will be able to apply this information on the test. If you've already seen sample questions for the test and you have an idea of the question format and style, try to come up with questions of your own that you can answer based on what you're reading. This will give you valuable practice applying your knowledge in the same ways you can expect to on test day.

Good luck and good studying!

Reading: Literature

Living on a Ranch

Marcus Morgan lives in Laramie, Wyoming, with his family. Laramie is between the Snowy Mountain Range and the Laramie Mountain Range, west of Cheyenne, Wyoming.

Marcus and his family own a large cattle ranch outside of the city along U.S. Route 287. The Bar M Bar Ranch raises both beef and dairy cattle, along with a small herd of sheep. Mrs. Morgan keeps chickens and raises a small garden to feed the family. Marcus and his two brothers, James and Robert, have to help with chores and taking care of the animals.

Life starts early on the ranch. Mrs. Morgan rings the bell to bring everyone in for breakfast at 4:30 am. The family eats breakfast with the ranch hands, and then the boys do their morning chores before heading off to school. When the boys return from school, they have more chores to complete before dinner and time for homework.

Everyone has a job on a ranch. Mr. Morgan supervises the ranch hands, oversees repairs, and takes care of all the vehicles on the ranch. Mrs. Morgan is in charge of paying the bills and making sure everyone is fed. Marcus, at 15 years old, is the oldest child and has the most responsibility.

He has to let the sheep out every morning and bring them back in every evening. He helps in the milking barn or with branding beef cattle when needed. He also takes care of the working dogs used all over the ranch. James gathers eggs, brings in a fresh pail of milk every morning, and cleans out horse stalls in the evenings. Robert, the baby of the family, helps his mom around the house and in the garden.

Marcus especially likes working with the sheep. In the mornings, he and his favorite working dog, Shep, run the sheep out of their corral into the big pasture so they can graze. Marcus uses whistles and calls to tell Shep where he wants the sheep to go, and Shep herds them. In the evenings, Marcus and Shep round up the sheep from the pasture and return them to the corral. Then Marcus must feed the sheep and check them all for injuries. In the spring, Marcus and Shep help Mr. Morgan bring the sheep into the shearing shed one at a time to have their wool sheared.

1. Where is the Bar M Bar Ranch?
   a. Cheyenne, Wyoming
   b. The Snowy Mountains
   c. Laramie, Wyoming
   d. The Laramie Mountains

2. How does Marcus tell Shep what to do?
   a. Marcus uses a clicker in his hand.
   b. Marcus uses a leash.
   c. Marcus lets Shep do all the work alone.
   d. Marcus uses whistles and calls.

3. Which of the following choices best summarizes the fifth paragraph?
   a. Marcus and Shep take care of the sheep.
   b. Marcus enjoys working with the sheep.
   c. Shep is a good sheep dog.
   d. Mr. Morgan sheers the sheep in the spring.

4. From this passage, you can tell that:
  a. Everyone has a job on a ranch.
  b. Children work much harder than adults on the ranch.
  c. Living on a ranch is no fun.
  d. Marcus does not enjoy his chores.

5. Mr. Morgan supervises the ranch hands and the outside chores. Which of the following choices best describes Mrs. Morgan's chores?
  a. She is in charge of the sheep.
  b. She is in charge of the chickens.
  c. She is in charge of the household and bills.
  d. She is in charge of the children.

6. From the passage, the reader can tell:
  a. Ten ranch hands work on the Bar M Bar Ranch.
  b. Working and living on a ranch is a full time job.
  c. A ranch in Wyoming is a lonely place.
  d. Mr. Morgan doesn't like sheep.

7. From this passage, the phrase "ranch hands" most likely means:
  a. The hands of people who work on the ranch.
  b. People who work on a ranch owned by someone else.
  c. The machines used to milk dairy cattle.
  d. A way to repair a fence.

8. Marcus, James, and Robert are different ages, but they have something in common in this passage. Which sentence best describes what they have in common?
  a. They all help with chores on the ranch.
  b. They all take care of the working dogs.
  c. They all have brown hair.
  d. They all have to shear sheep.

Geocaching

"Would you like to go geocaching with me this weekend, Tommy?" asked his father. "I have found a couple of new ones near the creek that I think would be fun. We could invite your friend Sam to join us."

"Sure, Dad. I love geocaching," said Tommy. "Should we go Saturday?" They agreed that they would leave Saturday morning to find the new geocaches, and Tommy ran to call Sam and invite him. Sam agreed to come with them. Although he wasn't sure what geocaching was, he always had fun with Tommy and his dad.

Friday night, Tommy and his dad got their gear ready. Both of them had handheld GPS units, hiking boots with good wool socks, a backpack to carry first aid gear, water, and swag for the cache such as plastic soldiers, a water pistol, and some playing cards. Tommy's father made sure that they had a compass and a map, bug spray, and hats, and he printed out the coordinates for the geocaches. Tommy had given Sam a list of things to bring with him, as well.

Saturday morning, Tommy and Dad picked up Sam at his house and off they went. "Mr. Jones, could you explain to me what geocaching is?" Sam asked, as they were getting in the car.

"Of course, Sam. Basically, it's like a giant worldwide treasure hunt. People hide geocaches, or containers, then take the coordinates with their GPS and enter the coordinates into a website where people like us can find them.

Then other people, like us, go hunting for these containers. Some of them are very tiny, just big enough to have a piece of paper for the date and your name. Some of them are large enough to hold books or toys and a logbook. Sometimes, people even put disposable cameras in them so you can take a picture of yourself at the cache. Sometimes, there are even items in the cache that can be tracked, so you can see how they move around the world."

Tommy's dad could see that Sam was still a little confused, but he knew that the boy would catch on as they got going. Mr. Jones put the coordinates for the first cache into his GPS, and off they went. "It looks like this first cache is only two miles from here," he told the boys.

The GPS led the trio to a small parking area just inside the local park, where they stopped and got their backpacks on, sprayed themselves with bug spray, and reset the GPS for off-road walking. "It looks like we have about 400 feet to go just that way," Mr. Jones said, as they headed away from the car into the woods. When they arrived at the location, Sam looked around. "I don't see anything," he complained.

Tommy laughed. "Our GPS is accurate to 15 feet, Sam, which means that the cache container is within 15 feet of Dad right now, but in any direction. The way we do it is Dad stands still, and I walk 15 feet from him. Then we know how far in each direction to look. Why don't I walk 15 feet to his right and you go left? Then we know exactly where to search." Sam agreed, and the boys quickly marked off their search area. "The cache is medium sized, Sam, so be looking for something like the plastic boxes your mom puts leftovers in, okay?"

Tommy, Sam, and Mr. Jones searched for about 10 minutes. They looked in tree branches, under rocks and leaves, and even inside of a hollow log before Sam yelled, "I think I found it!" Sure enough, he had found the container under a pile of leaves beside the hollow log. Since this was Sam's first find, Tommy and his dad let Sam open the box and choose an item to trade. Sam chose to take a bouncy rubber ball and leave a water gun. Mr.

Jones signed the logbook for all of them, and they hid the cache back where they found it.

"That was so much fun, Tommy! I'm so glad you asked me to come along," Sam said excitedly.

"Does that mean you boys are ready to find the next one?" Mr. Jones asked. The boys cheered and the three set off for the car.

1. Why did Sam go with Tommy and Mr. Jones?
> a. He loved geocaching.
> b. Tommy offered to give him a water pistol.
> c. He always had fun when he was with Tommy and Mr. Jones.
> d. He wanted to go swimming in the creek.

2. Why did Sam and Tommy have to mark off a search area?
> a. The GPS was accurate only to 15 feet.
> b. Tommy's dad wanted to make the boys work harder.
> c. Searching a big area was more fun.
> d. Tommy wanted Sam to learn how to search.

3. Tommy gave Sam a list of items to bring with him. What might have been on that list?
> a. A towel, a beach ball, and a sand bucket
> b. A raincoat, an umbrella, and rubber boots
> c. Wool socks, hiking boots, and a backpack
> d. Books, a flashlight, and a tent

4. Which of the following sentences is the best summary of paragraph five?
> a. Geocaching is a treasure hunt for small containers using GPS coordinates.
> b. Geocaching is a game for people to play online.
> c. Geocaching is about logbooks and taking pictures.
> d. Geocaching is something only boys do.

5. From the passage, "swag" most likely means
    a. How a person walks
    b. Small items or toys to trade
    c. A bag with money in it
    d. A backpack to carry your gear in

6. In the car, Mr. Jones teaches Sam about geocaching. Does Tommy teach Sam anything?
    a. Yes, Tommy teaches Sam about using a backpack.
    b. No, Sam teaches Tommy about comic books.
    c. No, Mr. Jones teaches Sam about drawing on a map.
    d. Yes, Tommy teaches Sam about marking off a search area.

7. This story is about:
    a. Two friends going into the woods for an adventure
    b. Two friends going geocaching with Mr. Jones
    c. Tommy teaching Sam about searching
    d. Sam learning how to use a GPS

8. From clues in the story, "cache" most likely means:
    a. A hollow log
    b. A path through the woods
    c. A pirate's treasure
    d. A hiding place

Dance Class

Jillian and Samantha attend dance classes at Ms. Suzie's Dance Studio every Friday after school. The twins have matching leotards and tights. They both wear their long brown hair up in a bun. However, that's all they have in common at Ms. Suzie's.

Jillian loves classical dance and is taking a ballet class. After she went into the classroom, she put on her satin slippers and began to stretch her legs at the *barre*. Jillian watches herself in the wall-length mirrors to make sure her feet are moving correctly on the wooden floor. When Ms. Suzie turns on the music, Jillian and the other ballerinas get into line and settle into position one. Jillian stood with the balls of her feet completely turned out, her heels touching and her feet forming a straight line. As Ms. Suzie took the class through the other four positions, Jillian thought about what was coming up later. Ms. Suzie had promised that today they would start learning *en pointe*. "*En pointe*" is French for "on the tip," when ballerinas stand on the tip of their toes as they dance. Jillian brought special toe shoes with her today, reinforced to support her feet and protect her toes.

In another classroom, Samantha slipped into her tap shoes and began to warm up on the wooden floor. Tap shoes are like dress shoes with little metal plates under the toes and the heels. The plates are attached by small screws that can be loosened to change the sound of the tapping. Ms. Jessica, one of Ms. Suzie's dance instructors, started the music. Samantha and her friends started working on their tap steps, watching themselves in the mirrors on the wall. Samantha started with basic tap steps, called single steps, and quickly moved through the different steps like the brush, the shuffle, and the ball change. Samantha likes the modern movements and music of tap. Jillian and Samantha both are practicing with extra effort. The school recital is next week, and they want to do their very best. The recital was so important to them that last month, their dad built a mini dance studio in the basement. It has a wooden floor, mirrors, and a *barre*. There is only room enough for one of them to practice at a time, so they take turns in the mini studio. Jillian practices in the mornings and Samantha in the evenings. They are really ready for the big night.

After class, the girls walked home together excitedly talking about their classes.

1. Why do Jillian and Samantha go to Ms. Suzie's?
    a. They want to learn to dance.
    b. They want to learn how to dress alike.
    c. Jillian talked Samantha into taking a ballet class.
    d. They just pass by on their way home.

2. Although they are dressed alike, the girls are very different. What is the big difference between them?
    a. Jillian has blonde hair, while Samantha's is brown.
    b. Samantha is wearing shorts, but Jillian is wearing a leotard.
    c. Jillian loves ballet, and Samantha loves tap.
    d. Samantha walks home, and Jillian takes the bus.

3. Ms. Suzie and Ms. Jessica both teach dance classes in studios. What did the two classrooms have in common?

     a. Both classrooms have TV's and game machines in them.

     b. Both classrooms have shoe cubbies and rugs.

     c. Both classrooms have wood walls and carpets.

     d. Both classrooms have wooden floors and mirrors.

4. According to the passage, ballet is:

     a. Only for girls

     b. Only for boys

     c. A classical type of dance

     d. A modern type of dance

5. A "*barre*" is:

     a. A bar of soap in the dish

     b. A bar of light through a window

     c. A bar of chocolate to eat after class

     d. A bar on the wall for stretching

6. This story mostly is about:

     a. After school programs for boys

     b. How much the sisters loved dance

     c. Friends having fun together

     d. How much the dad loves the twins

Island Ponies

Assateague Island is on the east coast. It is a long, thin island. It is so long that two-thirds of it is in Maryland and one-third in Virginia. The Maryland end of the island has most of the Assateague National Seashore and Assateague Park. The southern end of the island, in Virginia, has the Chincoteague National Wildlife Refuge.

Two herds of wild ponies live on this island. The ponies that live in Maryland are called the Assateague horses, and the ponies that live in Virginia are called the Chincoteague ponies. Standing only an average of 13.2 hands high, or 54 inches, they are considered ponies because of how short they are. Both herds look alike, too. The ponies can be either solid colored or pinto patterned. The two herds are the same kind of horses, but they are treated very differently.

The Assateague horses are considered wild animals. Unless there is a dire need, they are left alone to survive on the poor habitat available on the Assateague National Seashore. The rangers do not give them vet checkups, or teach them to ride or even like being around humans. They live as they have since the first ponies came to the island after a Spanish galleon sank off the coast in the 1500's.

A vet, however, checks the Chincoteague ponies twice a year. They are given shots and kept healthy, despite the poor vegetation on the island. The Virginia ponies are used to people because of this treatment. The Chincoteague herd is managed by the Chincoteague Volunteer Fire Department, which holds a very special pony sale every year.

Assateague Island isn't very big, so the herds have to be kept small so they all have enough food and room. Both herds average 150 ponies. To keep the herd that small, every year in July the Fire Department rounds up the Chincoteague ponies by using bigger horses to drive them into the water for the 10 minute swim to Chincoteague Island. The ponies are checked by vets, and then some of them are sold to spectators who want a pony of their very own. The remainder of the herd is allowed to rest, and then they are pushed to swim back to their home island.

The money from this sale helps the Fire Department buy new equipment and pays for the veterinarians who take care of the herd. It also helps to keep people interested in the ponies. So many people come to this sale and love the ponies that there was even a famous children's book written about one of the first ponies sold.

1. Which sentence best summarizes paragraph 2?
    a. Assateague horses and Chincoteague ponies are very different.
    b. Assateague horses are tall, while Chincoteague ponies are short.
    c. Assateague horses and Chincoteague ponies are the same breed of horse.
    d. Assateague horses are nicer than Chincoteague ponies.

2. In paragraph five, the word "spectator" most likely means:
    a. A ghost
    b. Someone who watches
    c. A special event
    d. A pony

3. How are the north and south ends of Assateague Island the same?
    a. They are both in Virginia.
    b. They are both in Maryland.
    c. They both have pony sales.
    d. They both have a National Park.

4. This story is about:
    a. Two herds of horses on Assateague Island
    b. Learning how to sell ponies
    c. How Firefighters raise money for new equipment
    d. Learning how to make ponies swim

5. Although both herds live on Assateague Island, they are treated differently. What is the main difference?
    a. The Assateague horses are trained for riding.
    b. The Chincoteague ponies are given veterinary care.
    c. The Assateague horses are all solid colors.
    d. The Chincoteague ponies are all pinto patterns.

6. How might this story be different if it was told from the point of view of a Chincoteague pony?
    a. The reader might think the Chincoteague ponies were all over the island.
    b. The reader might think the Assateague horses were a different breed of horse.
    c. The reader might think that the ponies were full-sized horses.
    d. The reader might think the firefighters were just being mean to the ponies.

Katie's Journal

Every day after school, Katie writes in her journal. She writes about what happened during school that day and uses the journal to help express her feelings. This week has been very hard for Katie.

Monday

"Dear Diary, Today was just horrible! Sandy yelled at me after band class, and I don't even know why! I am not going to be her friend anymore!!!!"

Tuesday

"Dear Diary, Jenny says Sandy said mean things about me today in math class. I just want to hit Sandy. Why is she being so mean? Tomorrow I have science class with her, and band again. I just won't talk to her."

Wednesday

"Dear Diary, I wouldn't look at Sandy today, or talk to her. Science class was very quiet and tense, since she is my table partner. I did say, when I was talking to myself, that I sure wished I knew why SOME people were mad at me and being mean. She just sniffed and walked away."

Thursday

"Dear Diary, Jenny told me that Sandy said she was mad at me because I took her music folder out of her locker and lost one of the pages. I didn't touch her stupid music folder, and I sure didn't lose any pages. But...I can understand being upset about losing my music. We play the same instrument, so maybe I can help."

Friday

"Dear Diary, Today I took Sandy a copy of my music folder. My mom copied all the pages at her work yesterday, and I helped Sandy find the one she was missing and we replaced it. Sandy said she was sorry for talking about me to Jenny, and I apologized for not speaking to her in science. She is my best friend again."

Katie felt much better on Friday afternoon, knowing that she had saved her friendship with Sandy. Writing in her journal always helped her to think things out and make better decisions.

1. This story is about:
   a. Katie having a fight with her friend Sandy
   b. Katie and Jenny talking about other girls
   c. Jenny and Sandy becoming best friends
   d. How science class was very hard for Katie

2. What is the most likely meaning of "tense" in Wednesday's entry?
   a. Relaxed
   b. Strained
   c. Dramatic
   d. Quiet

3. How would the story be different without Friday's entry?
   a. The reader would know that Katie wasn't a nice person.
   b. The reader would think that Jenny was trying to break up Katie and Sandy's friendship.
   c. The reader wouldn't know that the fight had been resolved.
   d. The reader would think that Sandy and Katie were acting childish.

4. How would this story be different if it were told by an adult such the Katie's mom?
   a. The reader would not be able to know Katie's thoughts.
   b. The tone would be more amused than angry.
   c. It would have more excited language.
   d. It would be emotional.

5. At the beginning, Katie was very angry. How is she different by the end?
   a. Katie was angry, but she became calm.
   b. Katie was hurt, but she became angry.
   c. Katie was amused, but she became hurt.
   d. Katie was calm, but she became excited.

6. Which sentence is the best summary of Wednesday's entry?
   a. Even though they weren't speaking, Katie and Sandy worked together in science.
   b. Even though they weren't speaking, Katie and Sandy gave a presentation in science.
   c. Even though they weren't speaking, Katie and Sandy still found a way to be mean in science.
   d. Even though they weren't speaking, Katie and Sandy both failed science that day.

An Artist Thinking BIG

A sculpture can be made in many different sizes, from very tiny to very large. The largest sculptures are carved from whole mountains!

Three such mountain carvings have been done in the United States. Two are complete, and one is still being carved today. One artist, Gutzon Borglum, has a connection to all three sculptures.

Borglum first worked on Stone Mountain in Georgia. The Daughters of the Confederacy, a group of women whose ancestors were Rebel soldiers in the Civil War, asked Borglum to carve a 20 foot high bust of southern General Robert E. Lee in 1915. Borglum talked them into a much bigger bas-relief, or shallow relief, project, but before it could be finished he fought with the Daughters and left. It was finished by Augustus Lukeman and Walter Hancock and completed in 1972. Although Gutzon Borglum did not finish this mountain, he developed techniques such as a giant magic lantern projector to cast a drawing onto a mountain. Later he would use this technique on another famous carved mountain.

The most famous mountain carving is Mount Rushmore in South Dakota. The mountain has the faces of four famous and beloved American Presidents. George Washington, Thomas Jefferson, Theodore Roosevelt, and Abraham Lincoln look down from an enormous mountain in the Black

Hills. Gutzon Borglum started the project in 1927, carving the four 60 foot high statues, until his death in 1941. His son, Lincoln Borglum, finished the mountain carving.

The third mountain carving is also in South Dakota, a short drive away from Mount Rushmore. The Crazy Horse Memorial, when finished, will be the largest sculpture in the world at 563 feet tall and 641 feet long. In 1939, Gutzon Borglum had an assistant artist named Korczack Ziolkowski working with him on the Mount Rushmore project. Chief Henry Standing Bear of the Lakota Sioux tribe asked Ziolkowski to carve the monument to show that Native Americans had heroes, too. Ziolkowski worked on the sculpture until his death in 1982. Now his wife Ruth and seven of their ten children are working to finish it.

Gutzon Borglum, and the artists that followed him, show us that no dreams are too big to become reality. One man, with the right vision, can change the world.

1. Which artist was connected to all three mountain carvings?
    a. Augustus Lukeman
    b. Lincoln Borglum
    c. Ruth Ziolkowski
    d. Gutzon Borglum

2. Which sentence is the best summary of paragraph 4?
    a. Mount Rushmore is the most famous of the three mountain carvings.
    b. Guzmon Borglum finished Mount Rushmore before he died.
    c. Mount Rushmore is the biggest sculpture in the world.
    d. Mount Rushmore has a hidden vault.

3. What do all three carvings have in common?
    a. All three carvings are finished today.
    b. All three carvings were finished by someone other than the original artist.
    c. All three carvings are bas-relief sculptures.
    d. All three carvings are in South Dakota.

4. In paragraph four, what is the most likely meaning of the word "enormous"?
    a. Small
    b. Huge
    c. Medium
    d. Unknown

5. This story is about:
    a. Three mountain carvings and the artist that connects them.
    b. How hard it is to finish a mountain carving.
    c. The artists who took over for Gutzon Borglum.
    d. How impossible it is for one person to change the world.

6. All three sculptures have common elements, but the Crazy Horse Memorial is different. How is it different?
    a. Crazy Horse is smaller than Mount Rushmore and Stone Mountain.
    b. Crazy Horse has no connection to Gutzon Borglum.
    c. Crazy Horse was finished by the original sculptor.
    d. Crazy Horse is the biggest and isn't finished yet.

The Disappearing Hair Ribbons

"I've lost more hair ribbons," Pilar said angrily. "That's the third ribbon this week that's disappeared." Pilar had beautiful long brown hair that she liked to wear braided with bright ribbons and bows on the end.

"Have you cleaned your room to look for them, Pilar?" asked Ms. Gonzales.

"I have, Mom, I looked under my bed and everything. Maybe if I ask Rosa to help, we can get to the bottom of this mystery," Pilar replied.

Rosa Morales lived next door to Pilar, and the two girls had been friends for years. Pilar and Rosa had started a detective agency last summer, and they had been hired by several neighbors to help solve mysteries at their house. The GoMo Detective Agency was becoming famous in their little neighborhood. Just last week, they had helped Marisol Lopez find her red rain boots.

When Pilar explained about her missing hair ribbons, Rosa quickly agreed to help. The GoMo Detective Agency was on the case!

"First, let's go to the scene of the crime," said Rosa, and they headed back to Pilar's bedroom.

Pilar had a four poster bed, a dresser, a night stand, and a desk in her room. She also had several pets: a hamster named Riley, a cat named Mrs. Piggy, and a ferret named Stinky. Riley lived in a closed hamster habitat with plastic trails to play in. Mrs. Piggy lived in the whole house, but she slept in Pilar's room every night. Stinky had a cage in Pilar's room that he slept in, but he was allowed to play in the room during the day.

"Okay, Pilar, I've got some questions for you," said Rosa as she got out her notebook to write down the answers. "First, who has been in your room since the first ribbon went missing? Second, have you searched all the furniture in the room? Third, where haven't you looked in the room? Fourth, what color are the ribbons?"

Pilar gave Rosa a list of the people who had been in her room. Mrs. Gonzales, Pilar's little brother Jaime, and Rosa were the only three people on the list. Pilar then told Rosa that she had searched all the furniture, inside and out, and even underneath! The third question made Pilar think hard for a few minutes, but there were only three places she hadn't searched yet: Riley's habitat, Stinky's cage, and the closet. The color of the missing ribbons was the easiest question. "One is blue, one is pink, and one is yellow," Pilar told Rosa.

The girls decided to search those places before they questioned any of their suspects. Riley's habitat was small and easy to search. While Rosa held Riley, Pilar lifted up his bowls and his house and ran her fingers through the pine chips on the bottom, but she didn't find anything. Next, Pilar held Stinky while Rosa did the same in his cage. She searched under his house, his bed, and in his food dish. The only place left was the closet. Pilar let Stinky run loose around the room while the girls searched.

Pilar took the shelves to search and Rosa took the floor. Stinky seemed to want to help too. He headed straight into the closet when it was opened. After a few moments, Rosa started laughing and pointed to Pilar's boots. Stinky's back legs and the ends of a blue ribbon were poking out of it.

GoMo Detective Agency solved another mystery!

1. What is the most likely definition of the word "suspects"?
    a. Someone who is thought to be silly
    b. Someone who is thought to be guilty
    c. Someone who is thought to be angry
    d. Someone who is thought to be innocent

2. Why is it easier for Rosa to think of the right questions to ask?
    a. Pilar is upset.
    b. Pilar is not as smart as Rosa.
    c. Rosa is older.
    d. Rosa is angry.

Read the sentences below. Choose B if the event happened before Rosa agreed to help, and A if it happened after.

3. Pilar's ribbons went missing.
4. Rosa searched Riley's habitat.
5. Stinky climbed in Pilar's boot.

6. What is the best summary of paragraph 4?
    a. Pilar and Rosa had been friends for a year.
    b. Pilar and Rosa were nosy.
    c. Pilar and Rosa were neighborhood detectives.
    d. Pilar and Rosa had been detectives since they were little.

Animals of Yellowstone

Jason and his family are visiting Yellowstone National Park in Wyoming. Jason and his sister, Jennifer, are hoping to see some of the more special mammals that live in the park. Jason and Jennifer love photography and want to take pictures of the animals. The week before their trip, Jason had prepared a chart so they could figure out the best places to look for each animal and how likely they were to see them.

Animal	Habitat	Likely Location in the Park	Population
Grizzly Bear	forests, meadows	Lamar Valley, Mt. Washburn, Hayden Valley, Mammoth Hot Springs	500 - 650
Black Bear	forests, meadows	Lamar Valley, Mt. Washburn, Hayden Valley, Mammoth Hot Springs	280 - 610
Gray Wolf	forests, meadows	Lamar Valley, Mt. Washburn, Hayden Valley, Mammoth Hot Springs	less than 100
Elk	forests, meadows	Lamar Valley, Mt. Washburn, Hayden Valley, Mammoth Hot Springs, Old Faithful	15,000 – 25,000
Moose	river banks, forests	South Entrance, West Thumb	less than 500
Bison	meadows, grasslands	Lamar Valley, Mt. Washburn, Hayden Valley, Mammoth Hot Springs, Old Faithful	less than 3,500
Big Horn Sheep	cliffs, mountain slopes	Mt. Washburn, Mammoth Hot Springs	250 - 275

1. Why did Jason research the Yellowstone Animals?
    a. He wanted to know which animals lived in the park.
    b. He wanted to impress his sister.
    c. He wanted to find out how many animals there were.
    d. He wanted to know where to look for the animals.

2. Where are Jason and Jennifer most likely to see moose?
    a. South Entrance and West Thumb
    b. Lamar Valley and Mt. Washburn
    c. Mammoth Hot Springs and Hayden Valley
    d. South Entrance and Old Faithful

3. Which animal has the largest population?
    a. Moose
    b. Elk
    c. Gray Wolf
    d. Grizzly Bear

4. Information in this passage suggests
    a. Big Horn sheep live in more areas than any other animal.
    b. There are more grey wolves than moose.
    c. More animals live in forests and meadows.
    d. There are more predators than prey in the park.

5. From the context of this passage, what does the word "habitat" mean?
    a. A regular or usual action
    b. An unfamiliar area
    c. A place where animals store food for the winter
    d. An animal's home area

6. What evidence does the author give suggesting they will NOT see any grey wolves?

    a. The wolves live in forests and meadows.

    b. The wolves have the smallest population.

    c. The wolves live in meadows and grasslands.

    d. The wolves can be seen in Lamar Valley.

A Day in the City

Robby and his dad planned to spend Saturday in Washington, D.C. They had several stops planned, including Pentagon City, Arlington National Cemetery, and the Smithsonian. Because it costs so much to park in the city, Robby and his father take the subway the first Saturday of every month when they have a "boy's day" together.

"We have to look at a subway system map and make a chart so we can figure out which one is the best to use," said Robby's dad. "There are five different subway lines in the city: red, blue, orange, green, and yellow."

	Red Line	Blue Line	Orange Line	Green Line	Yellow Line
Pentagon City		X			X
The White House		X	X		
Smithsonian		X	X		
National Zoo	X				
National Archives				X	X
Arlington Cemetery		X			
National Air and Space Museum		X	X	X	X
International Spy Museum	X			X	X
Washington National Cathedral	X				

1. How will Robby and his dad get to all the places on their list?
   a. Walk
   b. Bus
   c. Car
   d. Subway

2. Robby and his dad can use the subway chart to help answer which of the following questions?
   a. What time does the subway arrive at the White House?
   b. How much does it cost to take the subway?
   c. Which subway lines would you take to get to the National Archives?
   d. How long will it take to get to Pentagon City?

3. Which of these best describes Robby and his father?
   a. They don't like to drive in the city.
   b. They enjoy doing things together.
   c. They think the subway schedule is too complicated.
   d. They think the subway is dirty and crowded.

4. Which of the following places could Robby and his dad visit while staying on **the same** subway line?

     a. The National Zoo and the Pentagon City

     b. The National Archives and the Washington National Cathedral

     c. The White House and the National Air and Space Museum

     d. Washington National Cathedral and Arlington Cemetery

5. Read the following dictionary entry for the word "chart."

     Chart (*chahrt*) n. 1. a sheet arranging information into columns or tabs; 2. a map, especially a marine map; 3. a graphic representation; 4. an outline map showing special conditions or facts, such as a weather chart.

Which definition represents the meaning of "chart" as used in the passage?

     a. Definition 1

     b. Definition 2

     c. Definition 3

     d. Definition 4

6. What evidence does the author use to suggest that the Washington National Cathedral is a difficult location to reach?

     a. It is only on one subway line.

     b. The blue line has many more attractions.

     c. Robby and his dad are not planning to go there.

     d. It is near the International Spy Museum.

Family Names

Surnames are names that families share. They are passed down from generation to generation today, but this was not always the case.

Last names were first used in Europe during the middle Ages. People only had first names, so if three men named John lived in your village, it could get very confusing! However, if one John was a baker, one was an archer, and one was a barrel maker, you could tell them apart by calling them by their profession. John the baker became John Baker, John the archer became John Archer, and John the barrel maker became John Cooper.

Does your family name come from a job your ancestors had long ago?

Last Name	Occupation	Origin
Bender	Bow Maker	This name comes from the Old English word "bendbow," for someone who makes bows for archery.
Cartwright	Cart Maker/Repairer	People named Cartwright were early transportation engineers.
Fletcher	Arrow Maker/Seller	Fletcher comes from the French word "fleche," which means arrow.
Mason	Stone Worker	Masons built brick and stone buildings such as castles.
Parker	Gamekeeper	Parkers took care of the woodlands and wildlife, much like a park ranger today.
Saddler	Saddle Maker	This person made saddles for horses.
Steward	Manager	The word "steward" comes from Middle English and was the title of the person who managed someone else's estate or home.

1. What is the main idea of this chart?
   - a. To explain family names based on a person's father
   - b. To explain European family names from the Dark Ages
   - c. To explain family names based on occupations
   - d. To explain family names based on different languages

2. From the passage, the word "transportation" most likely means
   a. To move people or things
   b. To build ships
   c. To build wheels
   d. To ship items to another place

3. What evidence does the chart give to support the idea that last names come from occupations?
   a. Lists of famous people with those last names
   b. Lists the first person ever to use the name and their occupation
   c. Definitions of colors and their meanings
   d. Definitions and origins of occupational words

4. According to this passage, if your last name is Cook, your ancestor most likely
   a. Was a pig keeper.
   b. Was a chef.
   c. Was a candle maker.
   d. Was a beer maker.

5. Two of the last names are from related occupations. Which two?
   a. Fletcher and Bender
   b. Cartwright and Mason
   c. Parker and Steward
   d. Steward and Cartwright

6. From the passage, "surname" most likely means
   a. Manager
   b. Middle Ages
   c. Last Name
   d. Occupation

Meteor Watching

Every year in August, the Perseid Meteor shower is visible to the naked eye and is a favorite for professional and amateur astronomers, alike.

Many people like the Perseid Meteor shower because it happens in the summer when people are on vacation, the nighttime temperatures are moderate, and the weather generally is good. People have been enjoying this summer sky show for over 2,000 years.

Meteors are little bits of rock and ice left over from a comet passing by. The Perseid meteors are from the comet Swift-Tuttle, which passes by Earth every 135 years. The comet leaves a debris trail through which the Earth passes every year on its way around the Sun.

As the Earth moves through the debris trail, the meteors hit the atmosphere and burn, leaving streaks of light across the sky. The best time to see this light show is in the very early morning when the moon is setting. You need to be away from city lights, with a dark, open sky to see the shooting stars at their best.

1. Which of the following choices gives the main idea of the passage?
    a. The meteor shower is boring.
    b. Watching meteor showers in the country is easy.
    c. The Perseid meteor shower is a favorite.
    d. Watching meteor showers in the city is hard.

2. What evidence does the author give to suggest that the Perseid shower only happens once a year?
    a. It only happens in August.
    b. The comet only passes by every 135 years.
    c. People have been watching the shower for 2000 years.
    d. The weather is good for the shower.

3. From the passage, what does the word "debris" most likely mean?
    a. A collection of things
    b. A comet's tail
    c. Scattered fragments of rock
    d. The orbit around the Sun.

4. Both the Earth and the Swift-Tuttle comet orbit the sun. What is the major difference between their orbits?
    a. The Earth is a planet with an atmosphere.
    b. The comet has two names.
    c. The comet has a debris trail.
    d. The Earth takes one year to orbit the sun, and the comet takes 135 years to orbit the sun.

5. What is the best summary of paragraph 2?
    a. People have enjoyed watching the shower for 2000 years.
    b. People enjoy watching the shower because it happens in the summer.
    c. People enjoy moderate temperatures.
    d. People enjoy being on vacation.

6. From the passage, what does the word "moderate" most likely mean?
   a. Extreme
   b. Average
   c. Mild
   d. Nonexistent

Reading: Foundational Skills

Parts of Words

Many words in English are made up of small parts put together. These parts include a root word and possibly one or more affixes. Prefixes and suffixes change the meaning of the root word. The meaning could change a little or a lot, depending on the affix added.

Root Words

The root is the main part of the word. It has the most meaning in the word. For example, the word midnight has two parts: mid- and night. The root of midnight is night.

In each of the following questions, underline the root of the word.
   1. bicycle

   2. comfortable

   3. biologist

   4. refill

   5. prearrange

Affixes

Affixes are parts of words that can be added to the beginning or end of a root word to change the meaning. Prefixes are added to the beginning of a word. Suffixes are added to the end. For example, un- is a prefix that means "not." So, "unprepared" means not prepared. If you add a suffix such as -ness to the end of a word, then prepared becomes preparedness, which means feeling prepared. The affixes really change the meanings.

Prefixes

*In the questions below, underline the **prefix** and then choose the definition that most closely fits the WHOLE word.*

1. irresponsible
   a. very responsible
   b. great responsibility
   c. lacking responsibility
   d. kind of responsible

2. antifreeze
   a. a liquid used to freeze other liquids
   b. a liquid used to keep other liquids from freezing
   c. a liquid used to freeze ice cubes.
   d. a liquid used to keep food from freezing.

3. impossible
   a. not able to occur
   b. unwanted outcome
   c. able to occur
   d. desired outcome

4. mistake
   a. a happy thing.
   b. a correct thing.
   c. an excitement
   d. an error

5. prehistoric
  a. before historians
  b. before written records
  c. after written records
  d. after history books

Suffixes

Suffixes are affixes that go at the end of the word. For example, if you add -hood to neighbor, you get neighborhood. So instead of "a person who lives next door," you get "a community." Big difference!

For the questions below, underline the **suffix** *and then choose the definition that most closely fits the WHOLE word.*

1. properly
  a. in the right manner
  b. in a serious manner
  c. in the wrong manner
  d. in a silly manner

2. joyful
  a. feeling or causing sorrow
  b. feeling or causing happiness
  c. feeling or causing pain
  d. feeling or causing noise

3. scientist
  a. a person who does magic tricks
  b. a person who writes books
  c. a person who studies science
  d. a person who sings songs

4. musician
    a. a person who plays soccer
    b. a person who cannot sing
    c. a person who writes about sports
    d. a person who plays music

5. excitement
    a. a feeling of eagerness
    b. a feeling of sadness
    c. a feeling of longing
    d. a feeling of loneliness

Writing

Nebraska Pioneer Children

Life as a pioneer in Nebraska was not easy. Most families farmed and lived in sod houses or log cabins. They didn't have electricity or running water. These pioneers faced many challenges, and these challenges were hard especially for the children. Prairie farmers often could not afford to hire adult helpers, so they relied on their children to help.

Children arose early, while it was still dark, to begin their chores. Some chores even had to be done before breakfast. Different seasons called for different chores. Boys learned to plant and harvest crops. They hunted and fished to provide food for the family. Sometimes they gathered cow or buffalo chips to use as fuel for the fire. Girls helped with gathering eggs, cooking, cleaning the house, mending clothes and socks, and taking care of the younger children.

School was a challenge, as well. Many children were taught at home because they were needed to help at home. Without the children, the farm would not have survived. Children who did go to school went every day except Sunday, from October to May. That way, they could be home during the planting and harvesting seasons.

Eighth grade was the highest level, and all grades were taught together in one room. School supplies were scarce and expensive, so instead of paper and pencils, most students learned to write and did their lessons on slates.

For each of the following questions, be sure to use examples or facts from the story to support your answer. Edit your work for correct grammar and punctuation. Remember to include an introduction and conclusion.

1. Choose **one** aspect of life for pioneer children and write about what surprised you the most.

_____

_____

_____

_____

_____

2. Explain why pioneer children had to work so hard.

_____

_____

_____

_____

_____

3. Imagine you could go back to pioneer days in Nebraska. What three objects would you take with you and why?

_____

_____

_____

_____

_____

4. Compare and contrast the chores of boys and girls in a pioneer household. Why were they different?

_____

_____

_____

_____

_____

_____

The Olympics, Past and Present

The ancient Greeks started the Olympic Games on the plains of Olympia in Peloponnesus, Greece. The games were dedicated to the god, Zeus.

The first games were held almost 3000 years ago in 776 BC. Back then, the Olympics consisted of only one game, a short sprint called a "stade." Only men ran the race, and they ran in the nude. In fact, women could not even watch the games, much less compete in them, because the games were held to honor Zeus and therefore only for men. An olive branch wreath was placed on the winner's head, because the olive tree was sacred in Athens, Greece. .

The games were held every four years, and the period in between the games was called the Olympiad. For 1,170 years, the Greeks held the Olympics every four years. As time went on, more events were added, including racing, wrestling, boxing, equestrian events (such as chariot races), and the pentathlon, which consisted of five track and field events (long jump, javelin throw, discus throw, foot races, and wrestling).

The Olympic Flame began in the original games, as well. To symbolize the death and rebirth of ancient Greek heroes as well as the time when Prometheus stole fire from the gods, a flame was lit at the beginning of each Olympics and kept burning until the games were completed.

Unfortunately, the Olympics were banned by Emperor Theodosius II in 394 AD.

In 1896, a Frenchman named Pierre de Coubertin organized a new Olympic games in Athens, Greece. These games featured 12 athletic events, including a marathon. Fourteen nations sent athletes, and all the athletes were male. Women began competing in the 1900 Olympics in Paris. The Olympics continued every four years, but they did not return to Greece for another 108 years. In 1924, the first Winter Olympics were held in France.

Today, the Olympics still happen every four years, but they are split into the Summer and Winter Games. The top athletes, men and women alike, compete for medals—gold for first place, silver for second place, and bronze for third place. Furthermore, the Olympics feature both solo events and team events. An average of 200 nations and over 10,000 athletes compete at every Olympics now.

The Summer Olympics include events such as archery, baseball, boxing, cycling, diving, equestrian, soccer, gymnastics, and many more. The Winter Olympics have different events such as ice hockey, figure skating, snowboarding, bobsleigh, skiing, and a biathlon (skiing and shooting).

The Olympic flame still burns. It is lit at the site of the ancient Olympic Games in Greece several months before the opening ceremonies. A parabolic mirror is used to focus the Sun's rays and light the torch. Then, runners carry the torch around Greece and transfer the flame to the host country. Until 2008, the torch was carried through many countries before reaching the host, but today it is given directly to the country where the Olympic Games are being held. The final runner lights the Olympic Flame with the torch. Just like in ancient times, the flame stays lit until the games are complete.

For each of the following questions, be sure to use examples or facts from the story to support your answer. Edit your work for correct grammar and punctuation. Remember to include an introduction and conclusion.

1. Compare and contrast the ancient Olympics with the modern Olympics.

_____

_____

_____

_____

_____

2. Imagine that an athlete from the ancient Olympics could compete today. What events would he want to compete in and why?

_____

_____

_____

_____

_____

3. Why you think there are now Summer and Winter Olympic Games? Use examples from the text to support your idea.

_____

_____

_____

_____

_____

4. Pretend that you have to give a presentation to your classmates about the Olympics. Write your speech, using examples and quotes from the passage above.

_____

_____

_____

_____

_____

_____

Language

Prepositions

Prepositions show the relationship of a noun or pronoun to another word or phrase. They show direction, position, or other relationships. An easy way to remember is to think about a cat. A preposition is almost anywhere a cat can go.

For the following sentences, underline the preposition in each one.
1. Nick ran between Nate and Evan.
2. Nate leaped over Evan playing leapfrog.
3. Evan climbed across the monkey bars.
4. Nate ran toward the slides.
5. Evan and Nick rode their bikes around the block.

Conjunctions

Conjunctions are connecting words that connect different parts of a sentence.

There are three kinds of conjunctions. **Coordinating conjunctions** help to connect two equal parts of a sentence; **subordinating conjunctions** connect a dependent clause to a main clause; and **correlative conjunctions** are *pairs of words* that link balanced words or phrases.

Examples:
Coordinating: Nick *and* Evan went to the playground.
Subordinating: Nate can't go swimming *until* they come back.
Correlative: *Both* Evan *and* Nick wanted to ride dirt bikes.

For the following sentences, underline the conjunction and then write whether the conjunction is coordinating, subordinating, or correlative.

1. Nick and Nate rode their dirt bikes through the woods.

2. Evan waited to ride because there were only two bikes.

3. Neither Nate nor Evan can drive a car yet.

4. Nate rode over the ramp, although it was too high for Evan.

5. Nick wants to eat not only pizza, but also hamburgers.

6. Evan wants to go to the movies, but Nick wants to go swimming.

7. Nate would like to have hamburgers and pizza for lunch.

8. Either Evan or Nick can ride the larger dirt bike.

9. The boys will go swimming unless it's too cold.

10. Both Nate and Evan are in 5th grade.

Verb Tenses

Verbs are words that show action. For example, in the sentence "Nate ate his hamburger," "ate" is the verb because it shows what Nate did.

The tense of a verb tells you when the action takes place.
- The verb is in the present tense if the action is happening now.
- The verb is in the past tense if the action already has happened.
- The verb is in the future tense if the action is going to happen.

Examples:
Present: Nate licks his ice cream cone.
Past: Evan ate his hamburger.
Future: Nick will drink his soda after lunch.

For the sentences below, decide if the action is happening in the present, happened in the past, or will happen in the future. Underline the verb and choose the correct tense.

1. Nate and Evan will go to Vietnam this spring.
    a. Present
    b. Past
    c. Future

2. Their grandmother cooks pho noodles for the boys.
    a. Present
    b. Past
    c. Future

3. Last year, it rained every day they were in Vietnam.
    a. Present
    b. Past
    c. Future

4. The boys will visit Tran Quoc Pagoda this year.
    a. Present
    b. Past
    c. Future

5. Their grandmother lives outside of Hanoi, the capital city of Vietnam.
    a. Present
    b. Past
    c. Future

For the following sentences, write the verb in its correct tense in the blank.

6. The boys _____ (ride) the train last year.

7. Nick _____ (enjoy) watching the scenery from the train windows.

8. Evan _____ (read) a book if they take the train again.

9. Nate _____ (want) to fly last year.

10. All three boys _____ (play) checkers if they ride the train.

Capitalization

Some words need to be capitalized. There are rules to help you remember which words need capitalization. Capitalizing can be confusing, so a good rule of thumb is that words are capitalized if they are unique persons, places or things (nouns!), if they start a sentence, or if they are an important word in a title.

Some Capitalization Rules:
- The first word of every sentence
- Names of persons, months, days, holidays, countries, states, and cities
- Initials used in names and well-known organizations
- The word "I"
- Titles of books, songs, or people

For the following sentences, circle yes if the underlined word needs to be capitalized and no if it doesn't need to be capitalized.

1. <u>jenny</u> and Kim want to have a sleepover.

Yes

No

2. They have planned the party for <u>friday</u> night.

Yes

No

3. "Let me know if your <u>mom</u> says we can have it at your
house," said Kim.

    Yes
    No

4. "She will, <u>i</u> am sure of it," replied Jenny.

    Yes
    No

5. The next school holiday is <u>thanksgiving</u>.

    Yes
    No

6. Jenny's mom works for the county <u>judge</u>.

    Yes
    No

7. Her boss, <u>judge</u> Johnson, is very nice.

    Yes
    No

8. Kim's favorite band is Ben <u>folds</u> Five.

    Yes
    No

Punctuation

Periods, Questions Marks and Exclamation Points – Ending Punctuation

There are three main types of sentences: declarative, interrogative, and exclamatory. The ending punctuation you choose to put on a sentence changes the type of sentence it becomes.

- **Declarative sentences** make a statement. A **period (.)** is the correct ending punctuation for a declarative sentence.
- **Interrogative sentences** ask a question. A question mark (?) is the correct ending punctuation for an interrogative sentence.

- **Exclamatory sentences** express excitement or deep emotion. An **exclamation point (!)** is the correct ending punctuation for an exclamatory sentence.

Read the sentences below and decide if the sentence is making a statement, asking a question, or expressing emotion.

1. What time does the game start _____

2. I returned my books to the library _____

3. Mom is making your favorite dinner tonight _____

4. Jason, your house is on fire _____

5. Is Nate your best friend _____

6. I love you _____

7. Nick, can we play at your house _____

8. Mr. Kessler's store sells school supplies _____

9. Where is your bicycle _____

10. That boy stole my bicycle _____

Commas

Commas are punctuation, too. A comma (,) tells the reader to pause for a moment, but not to stop completely. There are lots of rules for commas, depending on the situation.

A Few Rules for Commas
- Commas separate a series of three or more words or phrases. (*She likes dolls, ponies, and kittens.*)
- Commas are used in dates between the day and year (*December 7, 1941*) and after the year if there is more to the sentence. (*On December 7, 1941, the Japanese attacked Pearl Harbor.*)
- Commas separate the name of a city and the name of its state or country (*Dallas, Texas*) or if there is more of the sentence after the state. (*We were in Dallas, Texas, last month.*)
- Commas separate two independent clauses before the coordinating conjunction. (*Sarah was hungry, yet nothing sounded good to eat.*)
- Commas separate a dependent clause from an independent clause at the beginning of a sentence. (*Due to a flash flood, we were not able to play street hockey.*)
- Commas separate additional information that could be removed from the sentence without changing its meaning. (*Joey, the boy in the third row, finished his homework.*)
- Commas show pauses in the sentence. (*Outside, the boxes were stacked in rows.*)
- Commas separate Yes and No and tag questions. (*Yes, I would like another piece of pie. No, thank you, I have had enough. It's true, isn't it?*)
- Commas separate direct quotes from the information that introduces or explains the quote. (*"Please don't forget to put your papers on my desk," said the teacher.*)
- Commas separate introductory phrases of four or more words. (*At the end of the month, we will meet our quota.*)

Write the following sentences correctly by adding commas where they belong.

1. In Houston Texas there is a huge rodeo in February.

2. Johnny said "Let's go play on the swings."

Changing Sentences

To keep your reader interested, you need to have a variety of sentences. Some of them should be long, some short, some simple, and some complex.

Rules for changing sentences:
- You can combine two short sentences by moving key words and phrases from one sentence to another. (*The aquarium is full of small fish. It is in my bedroom. Combined: The aquarium in my bedroom is full of small fish.*)
- You can combine sentence with related ideas to make compound or complex sentences. To do this, you use conjunctions such as *and, or,* and *because*. (I am happy. I see a puppy. Combined: I am happy because I see a puppy.)

For the sentence pairs below, combine them to make more interesting sentences.

1. Nate and Evan go to the Houston Zoo. They go on Sundays.

_____

_____

2. Dragonflies live by the river. I am hoping to see some today.

_____

_____

3. Evan likes the monkeys. The monkeys live in the primate habitat.

_____

_____

4. Baboons are from African and Asia. They mostly live in zoos now.

_____

_____

5. Nick watches the baby giraffe. It tries to eat leaves from a tall tree.

_____

_____

Multiple Meaning Words

Some words have more than one meaning. There are two types of multiple meaning words: those that sound alike, or those that sound different.
- Words that sound alike
    - Homophones sound alike but are spelled differently. (*I **so** want to **sew** that button for you.*)
- Words that sound different
    - Heteronyms are spelled the same but sound different. (*It's hard to drive a **windy** road on a **windy** day.*)

Homophones:

For the questions below, circle the correct homophone to match the meaning.

1. 9 minus 7	too	two
2. correct	write	right
3. not here but	there	they're
4. less than two	one	won
5. tossed	through	threw
6. make a mistake	air	err
7. walkway	isle	aisle
8. chewed and swallowed	ate	eight
9. deep or low	bass	base
10. uncovered	bare	bear

Heteronyms

Read the sentences below and circle the correct heteronym to fit the meaning in parenthesis.

1. The Polish furniture needs polish. (a substance to give a shiny surface)

2. I object to that object. (disapprove)

3. She was too close to the window to close it. (to shut)

4. The bass drum had a bass painted on it. (a fish)

5. Mr. Jones is ready to present the present to the President. (to give formally)

6. Don't desert us just because we are in the desert. (to leave)

7. The dove dove for the food. (a bird)

8. Give me a minute and I'll show you minute particles in my microscope. (tiny)

9. The singer is here to record a new record. (to preserve in sound)

10. I refuse to take out the refuse. (to say no)

Greek and Latin roots and affixes

Earlier, you worked with some common root words and affixes (prefixes and suffixes). Knowing what the root word means, or understanding the affix, can help you to figure out the meaning of a new word.

For the sentences below, the Greek / Latin root or affix and its meaning have been provided. The sentences use a variation of this root word. Use the meaning of the Greek / Latin word to help you place the correct modern word in the right sentence.

1. Photo = light

photograph   telephoto   photosynthesis   photogenic

a. She certainly is _____.

b. My new camera takes a great _____.

c. This big lens helps take _____ shots.

d. Plants use _____ to make food.

2. Aero = air

aerobics   aerodynamics   aeronautics   aerate

a. The study of wind flow over an object is called _____.

b. My mom takes a(n) _____. exercise class.

c. Poke holes in the soil to _____. the roots of the plant.

d. Scientist use _____. to improve plane and space flight.

3. Dem = people

democracy   demography   endemic   epidemic

a. When a lot of people catch the same disease, it's known as a(n)

_____.

b. America's form of government is a(n) _____.

c. The study of vital statistics such as birth rates is called _____.

d. A(n) _____disease is found in a particular place or people.

Context Clues

Learning how to guess words you don't know is an important skill, and one of the best ways to do that is with context clues. Use the rest of the sentence, or even the whole paragraph to figure out what an unfamiliar word might mean.

For the questions below, read the sentence and use context clues to choose the most likely meaning for the underlined word.

1. Robert's pet snake <u>slithered</u> across the floor.
   a. moved
   b. stopped
   c. hunted
   d. chased

2. We should <u>abolish</u> the "no hats" rule in class.
   a. start
   b. get rid of
   c. comply with
   d. agree with

3. I feel <u>deprived</u> when I can't play my guitar.
   - a. damaged
   - b. challenged
   - c. happy
   - d. denied

4. Wind Cave is <u>immense</u>! I can't see the top!
   - a. huge
   - b. small
   - c. damp
   - d. dark

5. The spy was very <u>nonchalant</u> as he walked slowly through the White House.
   - a. happy
   - b. sad
   - c. calm
   - d. excited

Reference Materials

Sometimes, to find the meaning of a word or learn how to pronounce it, you have to use reference materials. Reference materials can include dictionaries, encyclopedias, glossaries, or thesauruses.

For the questions below, a dictionary entry has been provided for you. Read it carefully and then answer the questions.

(1) **Miniature** . (2) [ˈmin(ē)əCHər]   (3)**adj.** of a much smaller size than normal
   noun. a thing that is much smaller than normal
   verb. represent on a smaller scale
(4)synonyms: diminutive, tiny, small

1. Which part of the entry tells you how to pronounce the word?
    a. 1
    b. 2
    c. 3
    d. 4

2. Which part of the entry tells you the definition(s) of the word?
    a. 1
    b. 2
    c. 3
    d. 4

3. Which part of the entry gives you words that have similar meanings?
    a. 1
    b. 2
    c. 3
    d. 4

4. Which part of the entry shows you how to spell the word correctly?
    a. 1
    b. 2
    c. 3
    d. 4

For the following questions, indicate which type of reference you would use to find the requested information.
    a. Dictionary   b. Glossary   c. Thesaurus   d. Encyclopedia

5. Where could you find out more information about Los Dios de Muertos?

6. Where could you find out the definition of the word *narrator*?

7. Where could you find words with similar meanings to the word *protagonist?*

8. Where would you look to find out the meaning of an underlined word in your science book?

Figurative Language

Authors use figurative language such as similes, metaphors, alliteration, idioms, and onomatopoeia to help the reader paint a picture in their minds.

Simile – compares two ideas, feelings, or things using "like" or "as"
>   *Ex: Float like a butterfly*

Metaphor – compares two ideas, feelings, or things without "like" or "as"
>   *Ex: The night sky is black velvet.*

Alliteration – repetition of beginning sounds
>   *Ex: Al ate apples all around Albany.*

Onomatopoeia – the words that represent a sound
>   *Ex: Boom!*

Idiom – a natural form of expression
>   *Ex: Out of the blue*

Read the following sentences and choose the correct form of figurative language.

1. I've been working like a dog.
>   a. simile
>   b. metaphor
>   c. alliteration
>   d. onomatopoeia
>   e. idiom

2. The dog barked and howled all night.
   a. simile
   b. metaphor
   c. alliteration
   d. onomatopoeia
   e. idiom

3. Don't buy that. Red scarves are a dime a dozen.
   a. simile
   b. metaphor
   c. alliteration
   d. onomatopoeia
   e. idiom

4. Geoffrey has the heart of a lion.
   a. simile
   b. metaphor
   c. alliteration
   d. onomatopoeia
   e. idiom

5. Suzie sells seashells by the sea shore.
   a. simile
   b. metaphor
   c. alliteration
   d. onomatopoeia
   e. idiom

Synonyms and Antonyms

Another way authors keep their readers' interest is by using synonyms and antonyms. This keeps them from using the same words over and over.

Synonyms are words with nearly the same meaning as another word. (reply/answer)
Antonyms are words with opposite meanings. (wrong/right)

*For each of the sentences below, write a **synonym** for the underlined word.*

1. The <u>large</u> dog jumped on the fence. _____

2. Math is very <u>difficult.</u> _____

3. Jack and Jill went up the hill with a <u>pail</u>. _____

4. Nate's dad was very <u>angry</u> with the boys. _____

5. "Don't <u>speak</u> to me," said Julia. _____

*For each of the sentences below, write an **antonym** for the underlined word.*

6. I love living in the <u>country</u>. _____

7. The cookie jar is always <u>empty</u>. _____

8. That dog is <u>ugly</u>! _____

9. You have to <u>freeze</u> popsicles before you eat them._____

10. <u>Throw</u> me the ball! _____

Practice Test #1

Practice Questions

Questions 1 - 8 pertain to the following passage:

A Garden in the Desert

1. Barry lives one street up and four houses down from his best friend, Manolo. Barry, his parents, and his older brother Ricardo have lived in the small ranch house for as long as he can remember. Manolo's family moved into their house a few months before Manolo was born. At that time, 10 years ago, their housing development was only five square blocks. About 250 small, one-story houses dotted the streets. Today their housing development is three times as big, and is considered an actual neighborhood. It is called Cypress Heights.

2. There are no cypresses or any other kinds of trees in Cypress Heights. The neighborhood was built near a desert. It has no heights and no hills – just flat stretches of paved road and concrete sidewalks. Grass sprouts up between the cracks in the sidewalks, but refuses to take root on lawns. Flowers also have a hard time growing in Barry and Manolo's hot and dusty neighborhood. The only plants that grow around most of the houses are patches of ragged-looking weeds.

3. In contrast to the dusty lawns, most of the ranch houses are very well kept. The outsides of the houses are freshly painted, and many lawns are decorated with bird baths and patio furniture. The lack of gardens and lawns, however, makes the neighborhood look dusty, downtrodden, and old. Without grass

roots to knit a protective net in the soil, the wind picks up dirt and blows it all over the roads, roofs, and sidewalks. After a windy day, everything in Cypress Heights is covered in brown and gray dust.

4. Manolo and Barry love living in Cypress Heights because their houses are so close, and each boy can easily get to the other's house. A short fence surrounds Manolo's backyard. Manolo can jump over the fence and walk along the path in the neighbor's backyard to Barry's street. From there, Manolo can walk past three houses to get to Barry's. The fence around Barry's backyard is too high to jump over and too smooth to climb, so Barry has to stick to the streets to get to Manolo's house.

5. One summer day, Barry rode his bike over to Manolo's house. He brought a backpack with a picnic lunch.

6. "Let's go to the playground at the school," said Barry. "I have two peanut butter and jelly sandwiches and two juice boxes for lunch. We can stay there all afternoon."

"Sounds good," said Manolo. His older sister was watching him while his mother was at work. He asked his sister, Rosa, for permission.

"Just be back before five o'clock," said Rosa. "Mom should be home by then."

7. Barry and Manolo's school was about a mile away. It was a long, brown, one-story building with big windows and a large play set in the front. In the back were two sets of train tracks. Usually, the trains only ran at night, but every so often a freight train would pass the school during the day, making the windows rattle and the children rush from their seats to watch it.

8. On their way to the schoolyard, they passed a house that had just been sold a few weeks earlier. On the yard, instead of dusty weeds, was white gravel. Dotted around the lawn were different cactus plants. Barry and Manolo stopped their bikes and stared at the lawn.

9. "It looks great," said Barry. "But I don't want cactus plants in

my yard. What if I ran into one while playing tag? That would hurt!"

"There are other plants that work in this area," said a voice from behind a large cactus.

10. A woman with short brown hair stepped out from behind the cactus and walked over to Barry and Manolo. She had a wide-brimmed hat on her head.

"We planted cacti because they don't need much water," said the woman with a smile. She waved her hand toward her house. "It is too expensive to water plants or a lawn. But there are other drought-resistant plants that will do well here."

11. "What kind of plant is 'drought resistant'?" asked Manolo.

"Basically, it is a plant that doesn't need much water," said the woman. "They include plants like lavender, aloe, lamb's ear, and oriental yew. I have some of those in pots ready to be planted. If you promise to take care of them, I can give you some to plant in your yards."

12. "Sure!" said Barry and Manolo at once.

The woman motioned to the boys to follow her behind her house. She put several small plants in a low, flat box attached to the back of her bicycle. She strapped down the plants and climbed on the seat.

"Lead the way," she said.

"Thank you," said Barry. "By the way, I'm Barry and this is Manolo."

"I'm Mrs. Juarez," said the woman. "Nice to meet you."

13. "Wait a minute," said Barry. "You just moved in. Shouldn't we give presents to you?"

"That's okay," laughed Mrs. Juarez. "I don't have any more room in my garden, so you are doing me a favor by taking them. But, I will take cookies if you have them!"

"Sounds good," said Barry. The three of them headed towards the boys' houses, ready to break ground on their new gardens.

1. Part A: What is the main objective of paragraphs 2 and 3?

Ⓐ To describe Manolo's house

Ⓑ To describe Barry's house

Ⓒ To describe Manolo's and Barry's friendship

Ⓓ To describe Manolo's and Barry's neighborhood

Part B: Give a sentence to support your answer.

_____

_____

_____

2. What is strange about the name of Barry's and Manolo's neighborhood: Cypress Heights?

Ⓐ There are no Cypress trees and the land is flat

Ⓑ The trees in Cypress Heights are actually oak and maple trees

Ⓒ Cypress Heights is located in a valley

Ⓓ There is no such thing as a Cypress tree

3. Which sentence in paragraph 3 showed that Cypress Heights residents care about how their houses look?

Ⓐ "The outsides of the houses are freshly painted, and many lawns are decorated with bird baths and patio furniture"

Ⓑ "The lack of gardens and lawns, however, makes the neighborhood look dusty, downtrodden, and old"

Ⓒ "Without grass roots to knit a protective net in the soil, the wind picks up dirt and blows it all over the roads, roofs, and sidewalks"

Ⓓ "After a windy day, everything in Cypress Heights is covered in brown and gray dust"

4. Why do Barry and Manolo like living close to each other?

Ⓐ Because it is convenient for them to visit each other

Ⓑ Because Barry's fence is too high to climb

Ⓒ Because their bikes don't work

Ⓓ Because Manolo has a shorter walk

5. What are "drought-resistant" plants?

Ⓐ Plants that can live in very hot climates

Ⓑ Plants that can live in very cold climates

Ⓒ Plants that can live in very dry climates

Ⓓ Plants that can live in very wet climates

6. Instead of grass, what did Mrs. Juarez put on her lawn to keep dust and dirt from blowing around?

Ⓐ Lavender

Ⓑ Yucca

Ⓒ Aloe

Ⓓ Gravel

7. What did Barry mean when he said, "You just moved in. Shouldn't we give presents to you?"

Ⓐ Mrs. Juarez was too busy to give presents

Ⓑ Traditionally, new neighbors receive gifts, not give them

Ⓒ Mrs. Juarez doesn't know Barry and Manolo well enough to know what they want

Ⓓ Barry and Manolo shouldn't take gifts from strangers

8. In paragraph 3, what does the word "knit" mean?

Ⓐ Join together tightly

Ⓑ Make clothing

Ⓒ Grow grass

Ⓓ Make nets

Questions 9 - 11 pertain to the following letter:

Thomas's First Complaint Letter
February 24, 2011

Thomas Goodwill
1234 Main Street
Thompson, Texas 77482

Romco Toys
8765 Madison Avenue
New York, New York 10008

To the customer service department:

I bought a Romco talking wind-up doll for my little sister from your website on November 12, 2010. The doll arrived on November 20. My sister opened the box on Christmas Day, and the doll worked fine until three days ago. At that time, my sister noticed that the winding part was getting harder to twist. Now it will not twist at all. The doll no longer talks.

My mom noticed that the papers that came with the doll state that it is guaranteed to work for one year. The papers also state that if the doll stopped working within a year, we should send it back to your company for a replacement. The doll is enclosed in this box. We would like a new doll to replace this defective one.

Thank you for your time. My sister looks forward to getting a new doll that works.

Sincerely,

Thomas Goodwill

9. Why did Thomas write this letter?
Ⓐ To invite a friend over for Christmas

Ⓑ To replace a doll he bought that broke

Ⓒ To buy a wind-up talking doll

Ⓓ To ask about a wind-up talking doll

10. How long is the guarantee for the doll?
Ⓐ One year

Ⓑ One month

Ⓒ Two years

Ⓓ Three months

11. What does the word "defective" mean?
Ⓐ Ugly

Ⓑ Definitive

Ⓒ Broken

Ⓓ Expensive

Questions 12 - 14 pertain to the following letter:

Romco's Toys Reply Letter

March 5, 2011

Customer Service Department
Romco Toys
8765 Madison Avenue
New York, New York 10008

Dear Customer:

Romco's wind-up doll was a very popular item with girls this Christmas. Unfortunately, many of the toys sold before the holidays had a defective winding mechanism that gradually became harder to turn. It made it impossible to operate the doll's unique speaking features. This defect is the responsibility of the manufacturers, so we are asking our customers to help the company recoup some of the loss it experienced due to this problem.

Included in this letter is a form we are asking all customers to fill out to receive a replacement doll. The form provides Romco with the documentation necessary to recover money lost from replacing the defective dolls. Please fill out the form and put it in the prepaid envelope provided. Romco will assume all postage costs for the letter and the replacement doll. After the form is received, Romco will send a new doll free of charge. Thank you for your concern in this matter.

Sincerely,

Romco Customer Service Department

12. What did Romco Toys agree to do for Thomas?

Ⓐ Fix the old doll and return it

Ⓑ Give Thomas a coupon to buy a new doll

Ⓒ Talk to the manufacturer about the problem

Ⓓ Send Thomas a replacement doll

13. What did Romco Toys ask Thomas to do?

Ⓐ Operate the doll's unique speaking features

Ⓑ Fill out a form and send it to Romco Toys

Ⓒ Write to the manufacturers about the problem

Ⓓ Buy a new doll

14. The following are five statements about the Romco doll.

I. Thomas purchased the doll on November 12, 2011

II. The doll worked on Christmas Day

III. The doll had a pretty voice

IV. The doll stopped working in February

V. The doll was cheaply made

Which of these statements is an opinion about the doll? Circle all that apply.

Questions 15 -18 pertain to both Thomas's letter and Romco Toy's reply letter:

15. According to both letters, what is the correct format for writing the name of a town and state in an address?

Ⓐ Anywhere. Texas

Ⓑ Anywhere: Texas

Ⓒ Anywhere Texas

Ⓓ Anywhere, Texas

16. Why did Romco Toys call Thomas "Customer" in its letter?

Ⓐ Romco Toys had so many complaints it couldn't write individual letters

Ⓑ Thomas did not write his name in his letter

Ⓒ In the letter, Romco Toys said it is standard procedure to not use customers' names

Ⓓ Thomas was not a customer; his sister received the doll

17. How long did it take Romco Toys to reply to Thomas's letter?

Ⓐ Two weeks

Ⓑ Two months

Ⓒ Nine weeks

Ⓓ Nine days

18. Tone in writing describes the feelings or impressions a piece of writing give the reader. Just a few examples of tone are happy, sad, polite, and angry. Which of the following best describes the tone of both letters?

Ⓐ Angry

Ⓑ Polite

Ⓒ Silly

Ⓓ Rude

Questions 19 – 28 pertain to the following passage:
Hobie's Journey across the Finish Line

1. "On your marks, get set, GO!"
While the crack of the starting gun was still ringing in his ears, Hobie straightened his right leg so fast he felt a twinge in his knee. He then swung his left leg straight in front of him. When he looked up, he was surprised to find himself nearly halfway up the track. His heart was thumping hard and fast in his chest.

2. "Go easy," Hobie thought. "You have three-and-a-half more laps to go."
He took a deep breath and lifted his legs slightly to relax his stride. His shoulders dropped a little as he swung his arms. Hobie's chest felt a little less tight. His feet tapped the track as Hobie matched the sound of his footfalls to those of the runners behind him.
"Try to save some steam for the end," said Coach Bennett. "That's when you can catch up to the jack rabbits that used up everything in the first lap."

3. Hobie loved going fast for as long as he could remember. In kindergarten, he was always first to cross the finish line during running races at recess. He won an award in second grade for running the fastest mile in gym. But every spring, Hobie chose playing baseball over track, despite his parent's pleas to consider track.

4. "You're such a good runner," said his mother. "And it would be so much easier because we would only have to drive to one practice."
Hobie's older brother, Martin, was a member of the county's local track club. Martin had joined seven years earlier and was now one of the team's star sprinters. But Hobie did not want to be compared to his brother on the track. Few people in the

town's Little League association even knew that Hobie had a brother, much less a brother who could run 100 meters in less than 15 seconds. Hobie wasn't the strongest player on his baseball team. He didn't like spending so much time on the bench, but he loved how he was always called "Hobie" or "Hobie Smith," never "Martin's little brother."

5. Three months ago, in March, Hobie was all set for his fifth year in Little League. He had been practicing throwing and batting after school. His aim was improving, and so was his throwing speed. Hobie hoped his efforts would mean he would spend more time in his position, right outfield, and less time on the bench. Then Hobie and Martin's father had an accident at work. Mr. Smith fell from a ladder and broke his leg and arm. He could not work or drive for six months.

6. "I don't have time to get home from work and drive to two different practices," said Hobie's mother, Mrs. Smith, to Hobie. "And it's not fair to make Martin switch to baseball after he's been in track for seven years and is doing so well. I'm sorry Hobie, but you have only one choice for a sport this spring, and it's track. You don't have to join, but if you don't, you're staying home with Dad."

7. Luckily, the coach for Hobie's track team, Coach Bennett, was new. He didn't know Hobie even had a brother. Also, Hobie turned out to be better at long distances. Coach Bennett had him focus on the mile and the 800-meters events. At the last meet, Hobie ran a mile in just under seven minutes.

"You keep that up, and I'm kidnapping you for the high school cross-country running team in the fall!" Coach Bennett joked after the race.

8. Hobie was now finishing his first turn with only two other runners ahead of him. He couldn't believe how well he had done this season. In baseball, Hobie always struggled to pay attention in the field. He loved batting, running bases, and catching fly balls, but hated the endless hours of waiting out in the field or on the bench for something to happen. In track, he

Copyright © Mometrix Media. You have been licensed one copy of this document for personal use only. Any other reproduction or redistribution is strictly prohibited. All rights reserved.

was always moving. And, for the first time, he was doing very well. He was the fastest distance runner on his team, and had won three out of the seven races he ran that season. Hobie pushed his legs a bit faster and caught up to the second-place runner. There was just one person blocking his view of the finish line.

9. Hobie felt his legs fly through the air and his chest start to hurt a little. He puffed his cheeks and swung his arms hard. Two more laps to go. Hobie kept pace a few feet behind the runner in the lead until they rounded the last bend of the track. Hobie drew a deep, ragged breath and started to run a little faster, making the distance between him and the other runner a few feet shorter. Hobie kept sprinting until he was running side by side with the runner in the lead. The finish line came into view. With his last ounce of strength, Hobie pushed past the other runner and swung his arms as hard as he could, flying over the finish line four yards ahead of the other runner.

10. "Good job!" shouted Coach Bennett, rushing out to jog alongside him. Hobie slowed down and leaned over to catch his breath, placing his hands on his knees. Then he looked up into the stands and saw his father waving his good arm. Hobie waved back. He was no longer angry that he couldn't play baseball. He was glad to be running track.

19. Why did Hobie choose baseball instead of track?

Ⓐ Hobie's parents wanted him to play baseball

Ⓑ Hobie wanted to avoid being compared to his older brother

Ⓒ Hobie was a better baseball player than runner

Ⓓ Hobie's brother, Martin, also played baseball

20. In paragraph 1, what does the word "twinge" mean?

Ⓐ Hurt

Ⓑ Bend

Ⓒ Break

Ⓓ Loosen

21. Which sentence from paragraphs 3 and 4 shows that Hobie is a good runner?

Ⓐ "Hobie wasn't the strongest player on his baseball team"

Ⓑ "Hobie loved going fast for as long as he could remember"

Ⓒ "But Hobie did not want to be compared to his brother on the track"

Ⓓ "In kindergarten, he was always first to cross the finish line during running races at recess"

22.   **Martin**   **Hobie**

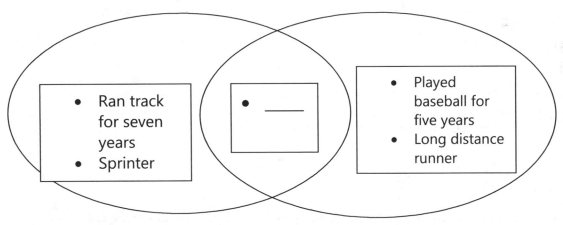

Which of the following phrases belongs in the blank?

Ⓐ Good at running

Ⓑ Older brother

Ⓒ Younger brother

Ⓓ Ran on high school cross-country team

23. What is the most likely lesson a reader will learn from this story?

Ⓐ Track is a better sport than baseball

Ⓑ It is dangerous to use ladders

Ⓒ Hard decisions can have positive outcomes

Ⓓ Big brothers like to be compared to little brothers

24. Increased tension or excitement in a story is called suspense. How does the author build suspense in the story "Hobie's Journey across the Finish Line"?

Ⓐ By describing how Hobie's father hurt himself at work

Ⓑ By describing how Hobie got better at running long distances

Ⓒ By showing why Hobie had to switch to track from baseball

Ⓓ By describing how Hobie got from third to first place in the race

25. Write a brief summary of this story?

_____

_____

_____

_____

26. What is the best definition of the word "ragged" as it is used in paragraph 9?

Ⓐ Roughly kept

Ⓑ Having a torn edge or outline

Ⓒ Worn-out from stress and strain

Ⓓ Wearing tattered clothes

27. Based on the events of this story, what is Hobie most likely to do next year?

    Ⓐ Join track as a sprinter to compete against his brother

    Ⓑ Join Little League and compete to be a pitcher

    Ⓒ Join track as a long distance runner

    Ⓓ Join Little League and play right field

This question has two parts. Answer Part A then answer Part B.

28. Part A: As used in paragraph 1, what does the word "crack" describe?

    Ⓐ A split in the track

    Ⓑ The sound of the starting gun

    Ⓒ The sound of a spectator clapping

    Ⓓ A hurdle that was broken

Part B: Based on your answer in Part A which of the following is an appropriate synonym for "crack"?

    Ⓐ break

    Ⓑ fracture

    Ⓒ split

    Ⓓ snap

Questions 29 – 33 pertain to the following passage:

Sticky Water

1. News flash: water is sticky.
This is a surprise to many people because water does not seem sticky. In fact, it's the first thing that people reach for to wash away stickiness and any other kind of dirt. The second item, of course, is soap.
2. Water and things like glue are sticky in different ways. Glue is sticky in two ways. Water is sticky in only one way. Glue feels

and acts sticky. It is used to join objects such as paper, wood, and plastic together. Water does not feel or act sticky.

3. Glue is sticky in two ways. One way is called adhesion. This is when glue, after it is poured on a surface, spreads into tiny holes and dents and hardens. The glue holds the surfaces together like the pieces of a jigsaw puzzle. But for glue to work well, it also needs to stick to itself and hold together. This is called cohesion.

4. Water does not have adhesion. If you pour it on a piece of wood, the wood will absorb the water, but water will not harden to make two things stick together. Water does have cohesion. Water is a unique substance made up of two elements: hydrogen (H) and oxygen (O). Water is made up of two parts hydrogen and one part oxygen. The formula for water is H_2O. The hydrogen atoms not only stick to the oxygen, but also to other water molecules, much in the same way magnets stick to metal. Water molecules stick to each other because of "hydrogen bonds." If water did not hold together, it could not be a liquid. It would boil and turn into steam.

5. To see the "stickiness" of water, try the following experiment. This experiment is not dangerous, and it only requires ordinary objects that you probably have at home. However, you will end up spilling some water, so ask an adult if it is okay to do the experiment before starting.

Sticky Water Experiment

6. You will need the following for this experiment:
One short plastic cup (the kind adults use at parties for punch works very well)
One small pitcher of water
At least 20 pennies
A sponge or rag for spills

7. First, fill the plastic cup with water from the pitcher. Make sure you fill the cup all the way up to the rim. Don't spill any

water! If you spill water, wipe it up. Make sure the very full glass is sitting on a dry spot.

8. Next, carefully slip a penny into the cup and look closely. Did any of the water spill over the edge? Probably not. Continue adding pennies slowly to avoid splashing. Slip them in gently. Do not throw them in.

9. Keep putting in pennies until water spills over the edge. How many pennies did it take for the water to spill over? It was probably more than you thought. Most people who do this experiment think one or two pennies will make the very full glass spill, but usually it takes more than 10 pennies. The explanation for this is cohesion. Each time you put in a penny, the water molecules hold on tighter and tighter to each other. Finally, when there is absolutely no more room in the glass and they're hanging over the edge of the glass, the water spills. One time, a scientist was able to get 25 pennies into the glass before it spilled! Now that's sticky water!

29. Why did the author start this article with the words "News flash"?

Ⓒ To show it is a news article

Ⓑ The author made a mistake.

Ⓔ To attract readers' attention

Ⓕ Because it is a news story

30. Which of these phrases belongs in the blank line in the chart?

Ⓒ Does not spill

Ⓑ Acts like a magnet on metal

Ⓔ Acts like water in a cup

Ⓕ Boils and turns into steam

Different Kinds of Stickiness

Adhesion	Cohesion
Sticks to surfaces Fills in holes Hardens Acts like a jigsaw puzzle	Sticks to other molecules in the liquid Holds the liquid together Does not harden

31. Why is it important that the cup is sitting on a dry spot?

Ⓐ To keep adults from getting upset about the mess

Ⓑ To make the experiment safe and clean

Ⓒ To keep the pennies dry before they go in the water

Ⓓ To make it clear when the water spills from too many pennies

32. Why did the author call water sticky?

Ⓐ Because of the way the water molecules are attracted to each other

Ⓑ Because of the way water sticks to surfaces

Ⓒ Because of the way water feels on our hands

Ⓓ Because we use water to wash up sticky messes

33. Which of the following choices is the best example of how water is sticky?

Ⓐ The force of gravity makes rivers and streams flow downhill

Ⓑ Water combined with soap is useful for cleaning

Ⓒ A paper clip can float because of the surface tension of water

Ⓓ Too much water in a cup will spill over the edge

Questions 34 - 37 pertain to the following passage:

Water and Keeping It Clean

1. We take water for granted. It is all around us in lakes, streams, pools, and oceans. We only need to turn on the tap to get some to drink or turn on the shower to wash ourselves with it. Water is everywhere. Most of the time we welcome having water, except when it floods into our basements or onto our floors.

2. It's important to remember that water is a valuable and life-sustaining substance. Without water, humans and most animals and plants would die within a few days. Water is also unique. It is the only natural substance that can be in three states – liquid, solid (ice), and gas (steam). For water to change from one state to another, it has to change temperature. To stay in a liquid state, water must be between 33°F and 211°F. Water freezes, or turns into ice, at 32°F. It boils, or turns into steam, at 212°F.

3. The freezing point for water does not change, but the boiling point for water changes depending on how high you are above sea level. The higher up you go, the lower the boiling point. So, water that will boil at 212°F by the ocean will only need to be 186.4°F to boil at 14,000 feet. That's good to know on your next hike up the Rocky Mountains!

4. Here is another fun fact about water. When it is in its solid form, ice, it is less dense. Ice, which is strong enough to hold up a full-sized truck on a frozen lake, is lighter than water. That is why ice floats.

5. Despite its unique qualities and its importance to our survival, water is almost constantly under attack, and the enemy is pollution. There are many things that pollute water, including chemicals in fertilizers that can be washed off fields and into streams when it rains. The waste we flush from our houses has pollutants. Most of it is treated at wastewater treatment plants, but a tiny amount still leaks back into lakes, rivers, and oceans.

6. The good news is that many farmers are changing the way they take care of their crops to prevent chemicals from washing into rivers. Scientists and engineers are working with wastewater treatment plants to make them better at keeping all pollutants out of lakes and oceans.

7. Even ordinary people can help keep water clean. Picking up trash helps keep it from blowing into nearby water sources. It is especially important to pick up plastic because plastic does not break down like paper and wood. Fish and other animals in the water get tangled in plastic bags. They may also mistake plastic objects for food, eat them, and die.

8. So, next time you are out for a walk or at a park, be sure to pick up trash and make sure it ends up in a garbage can. You will not only make the place look better, but you will also be saving the lives of animals in the water and keeping the water clean.

34. What are the three states of water?

Ⓐ Solid, liquid, gas

Ⓑ Gas, steam, ice

Ⓒ Water, ice, solid

Ⓓ Liquid, solid, water

35. What is the boiling point of water at 14,000 feet above sea level?

Ⓐ 330.2°F

Ⓑ 211°F

Ⓒ 186.4°F

Ⓓ 212°F

36. There are five statements about water below.

I.   There should be a stricter law against people who pollute the water

II.   Water pollution isn't the biggest problem facing the world today

III.   Fertilizers washed off of fields by rain pollute nearby streams, rivers, and lakes

IV.   People who pollute the water are bad

V.   Water is the only natural substance that can be found in three states

Which of the above statements are facts?

Ⓐ II and III

Ⓑ III and IV

Ⓒ I, III, and V

Ⓓ III and V

37. Which of these is a "fun fact" that the article gives about water?

ⒶThe waste we flush from our houses has pollutants.

ⒷThe freezing point for water does not change, but the boiling point for water changes depending on how high you are above sea level.

Ⓒ When it is in its solid form, ice, it is less dense.

ⒹWater is also unique. It is the only natural substance that can be in three states – liquid, solid (ice), and gas (steam).

Questions 38- 40 pertain to both articles "Sticky Water" and "Water and Keeping it Clean":

38. What is one idea expressed in both articles?

Ⓐ Water is a unique substance

Ⓑ All living creatures need water to survive

Ⓒ Water is wet

Ⓓ Water is sticky

39. How is the article "Sticky Water" different from "Water and Keeping It Clean"?

Ⓐ "Sticky Water" shows where water comes from and "Water and Keeping It Clean" talks about water pollution

Ⓑ "Sticky Water" mostly describes a property of water and "Water and Keeping It Clean" mostly talks about a problem related to water

Ⓒ "Sticky Water" is about cohesion and "Water and Keeping It Clean" is about adhesion

Ⓓ "Sticky Water" is a true story and "Water and Keeping It Clean" is made up

40. In what kind of book or magazine would these articles most likely be found?

Ⓐ English language arts

Ⓑ Social studies

Ⓒ Math

Ⓓ Science

Practice Test #2

Practice Questions

Questions 1 – 9 pertain to the following passage:
War: The Card Game

1. Rain came down in sheets, drumming on the windows and then splashing on the tiny deck that stuck out from Mona and Yuri's third floor apartment. Mona looked out at the yard outside the apartment complex. Large puddles were forming in the middle of the lawn, making a small lake around a tree where she, her brother Yuri, and the neighborhood children liked to play.

2. "I am so sick of this rain," said Mona. It was Saturday. Her mother, a nurse, was sleeping after working overnight at the hospital. Mona and her brother usually went outside to let her mother sleep, but the rain was so heavy that even with raincoats and hoods, they'd be drenched in minutes. They watched cartoons for a couple of hours, but soon grew restless. It was 11 a.m., too early to eat the lunch their mother had left them. It was also too early for their mother to wake up. She went to bed around 7 a.m. and didn't like to get up before 3 in the afternoon.

3. "Let's play War," said Yuri.

"War?" asked Mona. "Are you out of your mind? Mom is asleep. Running around the apartment and whooping it up will wake her in no time. You know how grumpy she gets when we wake her early."

"This is a different kind of game," said Yuri. "My friend Peter taught it to me at the babysitter's yesterday afternoon. You play it with cards."

4. "Cards?" said Mona. "How do you play War with cards?"

"Like this," said Yuri. He took a deck of playing cards from the dining room cabinet. "First you shuffle them. I'm not very good at that."

5. After Mona shuffled the cards Yuri dealt half the deck to Mona and half to himself. Then he put his cards face down in a pile in front of him and told Mona to do the same. He put his hand over the pile and told Mona to take the first card from the top of her pile and lay it down between them on the count of three.

"One, two, three!" counted Mona and Yuri. Mona had a five and Yuri's card was a six.

6. "The higher card wins, so I take this round," said Yuri, picking up both cards and setting them next to where he was sitting. Yuri explained that in the card game War, both players put down a card at the same time and the player with the higher valued card takes both cards. He explained that aces are the highest valued cards, followed by kings, queens, and jacks. Then the cards go by their numbers—10, 9, 8, and so on.

7. "What if both players have the same number?" asked Mona. "That's when you have a war!" said Yuri excitedly. "If you both have the same number, you each put down two more cards face down and then turn the third card up. Whoever has the higher card then takes all eight cards. We play until we run out of cards and the player with the most cards wins. Isn't it easy?"

8. "Yes," said Mona.

Mona and Yuri continued playing until both of them put down a jack.

"War!" they whispered excitedly.

They put down two cards and then a third card that they placed face up. Mona had a queen and Yuri had a six. Mona took all eight cards. At the end of the game Mona had 30 cards and Yuri had 22.

9. "I won!" said Mona excitedly.

"Beginner's luck," said Yuri.

"Actually, this game is all luck," said Mona.

"True," said Yuri. "Want to go best out of three?"

"You bet!" said Mona.

10. They played for the rest of the morning, until it was time to eat lunch. In what seemed like no time at all, their mother was awake and they were planning a quick trip out of the house.

"That was a great game," said Mona. "Thanks for teaching me, Yuri."

1. What does the writer mean by the phrase "rain came down in sheets"?

Ⓐ It was raining on the laundry

Ⓑ It was raining very hard

Ⓒ It was raining lightly

Ⓓ It was raining diagonally

2. Why couldn't Mona and Yuri run around the apartment and make noise?

Ⓐ The downstairs neighbor would be angry

Ⓑ There were strict rules against making noise before noon on weekends

Ⓒ Mona was sick and couldn't stand loud noises

Ⓓ Mona and Yuri's mother was asleep

3. What time was Yuri's and Mona's mother expected to wake up?

Ⓐ 7 a.m.

Ⓑ 11 a.m.

Ⓒ 3 p.m.

Ⓓ 5 p.m.

4. What kind of game did Yuri suggest playing?

Ⓐ A card game

Ⓑ A computer game

Ⓒ A board game

Ⓓ A running game

5. Which card has the highest value in War?

Ⓐ Ace

Ⓑ Queen

Ⓒ King

Ⓓ Jack

6. What has to happen in the game to have a "war"?

Ⓐ One player must have an ace

Ⓑ Both players must have the same card

Ⓒ Both players must run out of cards

Ⓓ One player must have a king

7. Who won the first game?

Ⓐ Yuri

Ⓑ Mona and Yuri's mother

Ⓒ Mona

Ⓓ Yuri and Mona tied.

8. What did Mona mean when she said "Actually, this game is all luck."?

Ⓐ The game does not require any skill to win

Ⓑ The game requires a lot of skill to win

Ⓒ Only lucky people win the game

Ⓓ A person needs lucky numbers to win

9. Mona and Yuri are playing War. Mona puts down a king and Yuri puts down a jack. Who wins the round?

Ⓐ Mona

Ⓑ Yuri

Ⓒ Nobody, because it's a tie

Ⓓ Nobody, because kings aren't allowed in the game

Questions 10 - 13 pertain to the following passage:

Ann Richards: The First Woman Governor of Texas

1. Born Dorothy Ann Willis in 1933, Gov. Ann Richards did not start out in politics. She taught social studies and history at Fulmore Junior High School in Austin. Then, she got married and stopped teaching to raise her family. While at home, Gov. Richards volunteered for political campaigns and causes. She worked especially hard to make sure people were treated and paid fairly.

2. In 1976, Gov. Richards successfully campaigned for the position of Travis County Commissioner. Six years later, she was elected Texas State Treasurer. She was the first woman in 50

- 103 -

years to be elected to a statewide office in Texas. She stayed in that office until 1990, when she was elected governor of Texas.

3. As governor, Gov. Richards worked hard to make the state government work better. She asked that the records and budgets of every state agency be looked at carefully, a process called an audit. She changed the way decisions were made for schools by giving parents and teachers living and working in the district more power to make important decisions. She also worked to make Texas safer by opposing, or speaking out against, dangerous guns called assault weapons. She arranged for more education programs at prisons so that prisoners would have more chances to improve themselves.

4. Gov. Richards appointed women and minorities to state government positions to increase opportunities within the state government for many different kinds of people. Gov. Richards served one term as governor. She lost in 1994 to George W. Bush, who later became president of the United States.

5. Gov. Richards was famous for having a great sense of humor and not being afraid to make fun of herself. She once joked about her hair being heavily styled by saying, "Neither snow nor rain can move my hair." To show that women were just as capable as men, she once said about a famous dancing couple, "Ginger Rogers did everything that Fred Astaire did. She just did it backwards and in high heels." Gov. Richards kept working to make peoples' lives better, even after she left politics.

10. What did Ann Richards do before she entered politics?
   Ⓐ Campaigned for the Travis County commissioner position
   Ⓑ Became governor of Texas
   Ⓒ Taught social studies and history
   Ⓓ Audited Texas state agencies

11. Part A: What is paragraph 3 mostly about?

Ⓐ Gov. Richards's humor

Ⓑ Gov. Richards's life before politics

Ⓒ Gov. Richards's first job in politics

Ⓓ Gov. Richards's achievements as governor

Part B: Which sentence supports your answer?

Ⓐ She changed the way decisions were made for schools by giving parents and teachers living and working in the district more power to make important decisions.

Ⓑ Gov. Richards served one term as governor.

Ⓒ She stayed in that office until 1990, when she was elected governor of Texas.

Ⓓ To show that women were just as capable as men, she once said about a famous dancing couple, "Ginger Rogers did everything that Fred Astaire did. She just did it backwards and in high heels."

12. Which word below best describes "styled" as used in paragraph 1?

Ⓐ method

Ⓑ fixed

Ⓒ approach

Ⓓ grown

13. What did Richards mean when she said, "Neither snow nor rain will move my hair."?

Ⓐ Her hairstyle was very stiff and strong

Ⓑ Her hair was very important to her

Ⓒ She used to work in the post office

Ⓓ She needed strong hair to be governor of Texas

Questions 14 - 17 pertain to the following passage:

Kay Bailey Hutchinson: The First Woman Senator of Texas

1. Kay Bailey Hutchinson was born and raised in Texas. She went to the University of Texas and graduated with a law degree in 1967. One of her first jobs was as a news reporter for a TV station. In 1972, Sen. Hutchinson ran for a seat in the Texas House of Representatives. In that job, Sen. Hutchinson worked with other representatives to make laws that would help people in Texas. She worked as a state representative for four years.

2. Sen. Hutchinson is a hard working person who has constantly worked to improve her career. In 1976, she was given a chance to be the head of a board that worked to find safer ways to travel in the United States. She left Texas to work on the safety board, which was in Washington, D.C. In 1990, she was elected as the Texas State Treasurer, the same job that Gov. Richards had been elected to years earlier. As the state treasurer she cut the budget and fought against additional taxes. Then, in 1993, Sen. Hutchinson won a special election and was awarded one of two U.S. Senate seats. In 1994, she won a full six-year term in the U.S. Senate.

3. Sen. Hutchison has worked hard as a senator. She worked to fix laws that changed the way money was spent for the military. She also wrote and helped pass a law that regulated shipping on the oceans. Sen. Hutchison also worked to give veterans and people who retired from the military health care benefits. In 2006, she was elected for a third time as a U.S. Senator.

This question has two parts. Answer Part A then answer Part B.
14. Part A: What kind of degree did Sen. Hutchinson get in 1967?

Ⓐ Master's degree

Ⓑ Doctoral degree

Ⓒ Law degree

Ⓓ Medical degree

Part B: What university did she receive it from?

Ⓐ Texas State University

Ⓑ Texas A&M University

Ⓒ Sam Houston State University

Ⓓ University of Texas

15. What did Sen. Hutchinson do for a job before she ran for a seat in the Texas House of Representatives in 1972?

Ⓐ Mother

Ⓑ TV news reporter

Ⓒ Lawyer

Ⓓ State treasurer

This question has two parts. Answer Part A then answer Part B.
16. Part A: What is the main topic of paragraph 3?

Ⓐ Sen. Hutchinson's life before becoming a senator

Ⓑ Sen. Hutchinson's accomplishments as a state treasurer

Ⓒ Sen. Hutchinson's family

Ⓓ Sen. Hutchinson's accomplishments as a senator

Part B: Give two examples that support your answer in Part A.

_____

_____

_____

_____

17. What does "Sen." mean?

Ⓐ Senator

Ⓑ Sent

Ⓒ Sentry

Ⓓ Sensor

Questions 18-21 pertain to both passages: "Ann Richards: The First Woman Governor of Texas" and "Kay Bailey Hutchinson: The First Woman Senator of Texas":

18. Why are Gov. Richards and Sen. Hutchinson famous?

Ⓐ They were the first men to be governor and a U.S. senator in Texas

Ⓑ They were the first women to be governor and a U.S. senator in Texas

Ⓒ They were the first women to be teachers and news reporters in Texas

Ⓓ They were the first women to have jobs outside of Texas

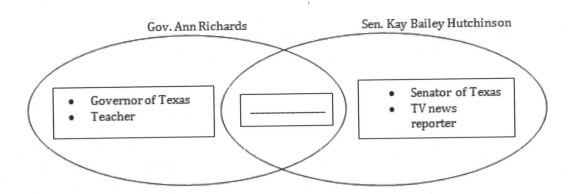

Gov. Ann Richards   Sen. Kay Bailey Hutchinson

- Governor of Texas
- Teacher

_____

- Senator of Texas
- TV news reporter

19. What word belongs in the blank spot?

Ⓐ Senator

Ⓑ Governor

Ⓒ State treasurer

Ⓓ News reporter

20. Which woman is still working in government?

Ⓐ Ann Richards

Ⓑ Kay Bailey Hutchinson

Ⓒ Both

Ⓓ Neither

21. Why do you think the author wrote about these women?

Ⓐ To show that women can have the same opportunities as men in Texas

Ⓑ To explain the way government works in Texas

Ⓒ To show Gov. Richards's funny side

Ⓓ To show that men have the same opportunities as women in Texas

A Trip to Pavarti's House

Pavarti and Sam are in the same fifth-grade class at school. It is almost Halloween and Pavarti invited Sam to come to her house that weekend to carve pumpkins.

Pavarti (answering the phone): Hello?

Sam: Hello, is this Pavarti?

Pavarti: Yes, is this Sam?

Sam: Yes. Mom said I could come to your house tomorrow. She wanted to know what time would be good to drop me off.

Pavarti: We're going to buy the pumpkins in the morning and start carving after lunch. Why don't you come around 2 o'clock?

Sam: Sounds good. Mom wants to know how to get to your house. What is your address?

Pavarti: We live in town, at 145 State Street. Where do you live?

Sam: We're just outside of town on Route 20, at the intersection of Townline Road.

Pavarti: Take Townline Road north toward town. After two miles you will turn right on Elm Street.

Sam: Okay, I'm writing this down. Two miles, turn right on Elm Street.

Pavarti: Good. You will pass two traffic lights. At the third traffic light you will turn left to get on Rio Turnpike. Go about half a mile until you see a 7-Eleven on the right. The next street after the 7-Eleven is Main Street. Turn right onto Main Street.

Sam: Wait, wait, I want to make sure I get this right. Left on Rio Turnpike, at third traffic light. Go right at the 7-Eleven, half-mile down the road. It is Main Street.

Pavarti: That's right.

Sam: Where is your house after I turn onto Main Street?

Pavarti: We're all the way on the other end of the street. However, Main Street is one-way and you can't get to our house from the other end. Go past five streets. Our house is on the right side, in the middle of the sixth block.

Sam: (Writing it down) House is in the middle of the sixth block.

Pavarti: Yes. It is yellow and has a garage on the left. It is between a green house and a white house. It is the only yellow house on my block. Do not look for the address. It is very small and attached to the door in a crooked kind of way. It's really hard to see.

Sam: Okay, okay, let me write this down. Only yellow house on the block, between green and white houses.

Pavarti: Right. And there will be one or two cars in the driveway. Look for either a red truck or a small black car.

Sam: I have it all down. Our car is a white minivan. Hopefully you will not see it go by your house more than once!

Pavarti: (laughing) You should be fine. If you do get lost, just call us: 555-678-9101.

Sam: Sounds good. Hopefully we won't need it. Should I bring anything tomorrow?

Pavarti: Just your pumpkin carving skills. See you around 2 o'clock!

22. What is the main purpose of the telephone conversation?

Ⓐ To arrange a pumpkin shopping trip

Ⓑ To give Sam directions to Pavarti's house

Ⓒ To arrange a Halloween party at Sam's house

Ⓓ To give Pavarti directions to Sam's house

23. Pavarti is having Sam over. Why did Pavarti ask Sam where she lived?

Ⓐ So Pavarti could give Sam directions from her own house

Ⓑ So Pavarti could someday go to Sam's house

Ⓒ So Pavarti could find out whether Sam lives in town

Ⓓ So Pavarti could give directions to the closest 7-Eleven store

24. After Townline Road, what street does Sam's mother need to turn right onto?

Ⓐ Rio Turnpike

Ⓑ Main Street

Ⓒ Route 20

Ⓓ Elm Street

25. Why did Pavarti tell Sam the color of her house and the colors of the houses next to it instead of letting Sam use the address?

Ⓐ Because the address is hard to see from the road

Ⓑ Because Sam cannot read numbers

Ⓒ Because Pavarti does not know her address

Ⓓ Because the address is easy to see from the road

26. According to Pavarti, what direction should Sam's mother take if she enters at the bottom of the Rio Turnpike shown below?

Ⓐ Straight, then right

Ⓑ Left, then straight

Ⓒ Straight, then left

Ⓓ Left, then right

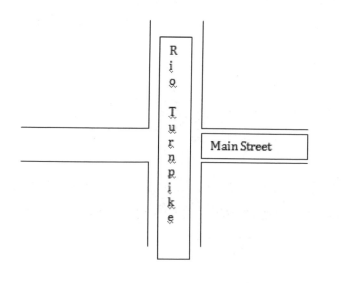

27. Pavarti told Sam to look for a _____ truck or a _____ black car. Choose the answer that correctly fills in the blanks.

Ⓒ red, black

Ⓓ black, small

Ⓔ red, small

Ⓕ black, red

28. What did Sam mean when she said about her family's white minivan, "Hopefully you won't see it go by more than once!"?

Ⓒ Sam is hoping they don't drive the wrong way on Main Street

Ⓓ Sam is hoping they don't get lost and have to drive up and down Main Street

Ⓔ Sam is hoping Pavarti sees their car go by once

Ⓕ Sam is hoping the car doesn't break down

29. Sam wrote down the following notes while Pavarti was giving directions:

- *3 traf lghts. L on Rio Turnpk*
- *7-Eleven on right, 1/2-mile down*
- *Main Street*

What part of Pavarti's directions did Sam write down?

Ⓒ Take Townline Road north towards town. After two miles you will turn right on Elm Street

Ⓓ It is yellow and has a garage on the left. It is between a green house and a white house. It is the only yellow house on my block

Ⓔ Main Street is one way and you can't get to our house from the other end. Go past five streets

Ⓕ At the third traffic light you will turn left onto Rio Turnpike. Go about half a mile until you see a 7-Eleven on the right. The next street after the 7-Eleven is Main Street

30. The following is Pavarti's morning schedule. What activity goes in the blank space?

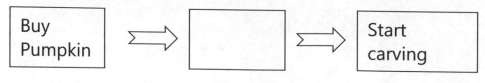

Ⓐ Take a nap

Ⓑ Pick up Sam

Ⓒ Give Sam directions

Ⓓ Have lunch

Questions 31 – 34 pertain to the following passage:
   Simon and Pedro's Shopping Trip

1. "Simon, where are you going?" asked Pedro. "You're missing your favorite show."

Pedro had just arrived at Simon's house on his bicycle. He had ridden over to see what his best friend was doing on a Saturday morning at 10 o'clock. Simon was usually watching cartoons around this time.

"I'm heading to the store," said Simon. "I've saved my allowance and I finally have enough money to buy the model plane I've wanted."

2. "Great!" said Pedro. "Can I come with you? I want to see it. Also, can I help you build it when we get back?"

"Sure," said Simon. "Let's go!"

3. Simon and Pedro rode down the street and turned right onto the highway. The hobby store, which sold model planes, cars, and other model vehicles, was just a few hundred yards down the road. At the store Simon and Pedro took some time to look at the other models on the shelves.

4. "Look!" said Pedro. "Here is a 1969 Mustang! It's $40! My dad said my grandfather used to own a real one. He bought it new and kept it for years. Then his brother, my uncle, bought it from him. Dad wishes he had never sold it."

5. "Really?" said Simon. "I'd love to ride in one of those. Look at this! A C17! Man, I'd get this instead, but it's $50 and I only have $30."

"What kind of plane were you planning to buy?" asked Pedro.

"The model of that B17G Flying Fortress," said Simon. "I have just enough to buy it."

"How much is it?" asked Pedro.

"It costs about $25," said Simon. "But I also have to pay for the sales tax."

"How much is tax?" asked Pedro.

"Eight percent," said Simon. "My mom figured it out for me. It's $2. That leaves me with $3 change."

"Do you get everything you need in the kit...like glue?" asked Pedro.

"Good question," said Simon. "I'll ask."

6. Simon went over to the clerk with the model airplane box in his hands. Pedro watched as the clerk nodded. He was hopeful that meant good news.

"Yes," said Simon, walking back to Pedro. "Everything is included."

"Well," said Pedro. "Let's head home and start building! When we're done, we'll break open my piggy bank and go buy the 1969 Mustang. Then we can play car chase."

"Excellent!" said Simon, as he headed toward the counter with the box and his wallet.

This question has two parts. Answer Part A, then answer Part B.

31. Part A: What was the model that Pedro noticed in the store?

Ⓐ C17

Ⓑ B17G Flying Fortress

Ⓒ 1969 Mustang

Ⓓ A18H Flying Dutchman

Part B: Why did Pedro like that model so much?

   Ⓐ It was the cheapest one

   Ⓑ His grandfather had owned a real one

   Ⓒ It was the easiest to build

   Ⓓ His grandfather loved airplanes

32. What model did Simon want to buy, but couldn't afford?

   Ⓐ C17

   Ⓑ B17G Flying Fortress

   Ⓒ 1969 Mustang

   Ⓓ A18H Flying Dutchman

33. How much will Simon's model cost with tax?

   Ⓐ $25

   Ⓑ $27

   Ⓒ $45

   Ⓓ $50

34. What did Simon and Pedro plan to do after Simon bought his model?

   Ⓐ Buy the 1969 Mustang too and build both of them together

   Ⓑ Build the 1969 Mustang and then build the C17

   Ⓒ Build the B17G Flying Fortress and then go buy the 1969 Mustang

   Ⓓ Buy the 1969 Mustang and then build the B17G Flying Fortress

Questions 35 – 36 pertain to the following passage:

Simon and His Father

1. "Well, that about does it," said Simon, gluing the last decal on the rudder of his model B17G Flying Fortress plane.
"We have to let the glue dry," said Pedro, looking down at the finished plane.
"While we're waiting, let's go get your car," said Simon. "It's only 3 o'clock, so the store is still open."
2. "I'll go home and get my money," said Pedro.
While Pedro was getting his money, Simon looked at his newly finished plane. He and Pedro had spent about four hours building it. Around an hour ago, Simon's father came upstairs with sandwiches and glasses of milk.
3. "Thought you two would like something to eat," said Simon's father, placing the tray on Simon's bed. "I'd eat this away from the work area, though. You do not want to get modeling glue on your lunch."
4. Simon and Pedro laughed while rushing to the bathroom to wash the glue from their hands. It was the first time Simon had ever built a model airplane without his father's help. His father had offered, but this time Simon said he wanted to try it on his own. Then, when Pedro asked to stay and work with him, Simon decided that he could use Pedro's help. Pedro read the directions and handed Simon parts while Simon looked over Pedro's shoulder at the plans and carefully glued the pieces in place. It was the hardest model Simon had ever built. Just then

there was a knock on the door.

5. "Can I come in?" asked Simon's father.

"Sure," said Simon. "Check out the plane!"

"Wow," said Simon's father quietly, looking closely at the finished model. "You and Pedro did a great job. It looks just like the real thing."

6. At that moment it occurred to Simon that his father, behind the proud smile, might feel hurt because Simon let Pedro help him after telling his father he wanted to build it alone.

"You're not mad?" Simon asked.

"Mad?" asked Simon's father. "Mad? About what?"

7. "That I asked Pedro to help me after you offered," said Simon, taking his eyes from his father's face and looking at the model.

"Simon," said his father, "of course I'm not mad. I'm proud. You and Pedro did a great job! I think I can take some credit for teaching you, but this shows that you are ready to start tackling these kinds of projects on your own. Or, of course, with a friend."

8. "Thanks, Dad," said Simon, giving his father a hug. "You did teach me a lot of things. I remembered a few of them when we were building the plane. Pedro knows a lot too. I'll probably get him to help me with the next model I build. Pedro's dad likes building models too."

9. "Speaking of Pedro, there's the doorbell," said Simon's father, giving Simon a quick last squeeze. "Would you two like a ride to the store this time? Traffic is pretty heavy this time of day."

"Yes, the traffic probably would be a lot worse now, so we could use a ride" said Simon. "Thanks, Dad."

"No problem," said Simon's father. "I'll get the keys."

35. Why did Simon think his father would be angry?

Ⓐ Because Simon didn't buy the 1969 Mustang

Ⓑ Because Simon's father didn't want to help build the model

Ⓒ Because Simon and Pedro made a big mess

Ⓓ Because Simon asked Pedro instead of his father to help

This question has two parts. Answer Part A then answer Part B.

36. Part A: What will Simon likely do the next time he builds a model?

Ⓐ Ask his father for help

Ⓑ Invite Pedro over to help

Ⓒ Read the directions more carefully

Ⓓ Build it alone

Part B: What sentence supports your answer in Part A?

Ⓐ I'll probably get him to help me with the next model I build.

Ⓑ I think I can take some credit for teaching you, but this shows that you are ready to start tackling these kinds of projects on your own.

Ⓒ I remembered a few of them when we were building the plane.

Ⓓ "Would you two like a ride to the store this time?

Questions 37 – 40 pertain to both passages: "Simon and Pedro's Shopping Trip" and "Simon and His Father":

37. From these two reading passages, it appears that Simon and Pedro are

Ⓐ Classmates

Ⓑ Enemies

Ⓒ Acquaintances

Ⓓ Friends

38. What kind of help does Simon accept from his father in "Simon and His Father"?

Ⓐ Simon lets his father drive him and Pedro to the store

Ⓑ Simon lets his father make dinner for him and Pedro

Ⓒ Simon lets his father help with Pedro's 1969 Mustang

Ⓓ Simon lets his father drive Pedro back to his house

39. What did Simon learn about his father in "Simon and His Father"?

Ⓐ That his father is a good cook

Ⓑ That his father is a good teacher

Ⓒ That his father understands that Simon and Pedro are friends

Ⓓ That his father understands that Simon is growing up

40. Why does Simon accept his father's offer of help?

Ⓐ Because he was tired from the trip that morning

Ⓑ Because Pedro was taking a long time to get back

Ⓒ Because traffic in the afternoon is heavier than in the morning

Ⓓ Because it was getting late and the store was going to close soon

Thank You

We at Mometrix would like to extend our heartfelt thanks to you, our friend and patron, for allowing us to play a part in your journey. It is a privilege to serve people from all walks of life who are unified in their commitment to building the best future they can for themselves.

The preparation you devote to these important testing milestones may be the most valuable educational opportunity you have for making a real difference in your life. We encourage you to put your heart into it—that feeling of succeeding, overcoming, and yes, conquering will be well worth the hours you've invested.

We want to hear your story, your struggles and your successes, and if you see any opportunities for us to improve our materials so we can help others even more effectively in the future, please share that with us as well. **The team at Mometrix would be absolutely thrilled to hear from you!** So please, send us an email (support@mometrix.com) and let's stay in touch.

Additional Bonus Material

Due to our efforts to try to keep this book to a manageable length, we've created a link that will give you access to all of your additional bonus material.

Please visit http://www.mometrix.com/bonus948/fsag5elawb to access the information.

GUARANTEED TO IMPROVE YOUR SCORE

"Effective, Affordable, Guaranteed"

At Mometrix, we think differently about tests. We believe you can perform better on your exam by implementing a few critical strategies and focusing your study time on what's most important. With so many demands on your time, you probably don't have months to spend preparing for an exam that holds the key to your future. Our team of testing experts devote hours upon hours to painstakingly review piles of content and boil it all down to the critical concepts that are most likely to be on your exam. **We do a lot of work cutting through the fluff to give you what you need the most to perform well on the exam.** But you don't have to take our word for it; here is what some of our customers have to say:

"I've just retaken my test and I scored way better than my previous score. I had this program for only 3 days and I just want to say that I can't believe how well it worked." - Mandy C.

"Just wanted to say thank you. Due to your product I was able to ace my exam with very little effort. Your tricks did the trick. Thanks again, and I would recommend this product to anyone." - Erich L.

"Just dropping you a note to let you know that I am completely satisfied with the product. I had already taken the test once and landed in the 75th percentile of those taking it with me. I took the test a second time and used some of your tips and raised my score to the 97th percentile. Thanks for my much improved score." - Denise W.

"I just wanted to tell you I had ordered your study guide, and I finally aced the test after taking it numerous times. I tried tutors and all sorts of study guides and nothing helped. Your guide did the job and got me the score I needed! Thank you!" - Nicholas R.

We offer study materials for over 1000 different standardized exams, including:

College Entrance Exams   **Teacher Certification Exams**
Medical/Nursing Exams   **Insurance Exams**
Financial Exams   **Dental Exams**
Military Exams   **Graduate & Professional School Exams**

For questions about bulk discounts or ordering through your company/institution, contact our Institutional Sales Department at 888-248-1219 or sales@mometrix.com.

Visit www.MometrixCatalog.com for our full list of products and services.

Made in USA

Mometrix utilizes a state-of-the-art, European-engineered square-fold mechanical book binding process, which avoids the use of chemical-based glues and minimizes energy consumption in the manufacturing process.

ISBN: 978-1-5167-0068-4

Florida

State Assessments Grade 5 English Language Arts

SUCCESS STRATEGIES

Teacher Answer Key

FSA Test Review for the
Florida Standards Assessments

**Guaranteed to Inspire
Academic Success**

Mometrix TEST PREPARATION

TABLE OF CONTENTS

Workbook Answers

Reading: Literature

Living on a Ranch
1. C - The Bar M Bar Ranch is in Laramie, Wyoming
2. D - Marcus uses whistles and calls.
3. B - Marcus enjoys working with the sheep.
4. A - Everyone has a job on a ranch.
5. C - She is in charge of the household and bills.
6. B - Working and living on a ranch is a full time job.
7. B - People who work on a ranch owned by someone else.
8. A - They all help with chores on the ranch.

Geocaching
1. C - He always has fun when he was with Tommy and Mr. Jones.
2. A - The GPS was only accurate to 15 feet.
3. C - wool socks, hiking boots, and a backpack
4. A - Geocaching is a treasure hunt for small containers using GPS coordinates.
5. B - small items or toys to trade
6. D - Yes, Tommy teaches Sam about marking off a search area.
7. B - two friends going Geocaching with Mr. Jones
8. D - a hiding place

Dance Class
1. A - They want to learn to dance.
2. C - Jillian loves ballet, and Samantha loves tap.
3. D - Both classrooms have wooden floors and mirrors.
4. C - a classical type of dance
5. D - a bar on the wall for stretching
6. B - how much the sisters loved dance

Island Ponies
1. C - Assateague horses and Chincoteague ponies are the same breed of horse.
2. B - someone who watches
3. D - They both have a National Park.
4. A - two herds of horses on Assateague Island
5. B - The Chincoteague ponies are given veterinary care.
6. D - The reader might think the firefighters were just being mean to the ponies.

Katie's Journal
1. A - Katie having a fight with her friend Sandy.
2. B - strained
3. C - The reader wouldn't know that the fight had been resolved.
4. A - The reader would not be able to know Katie's thoughts.
5. A - Katie was angry, but she became calm.
6. C - Even though they weren't speaking, Katie and Sandy still found a way to be mean in science.

An Artist Thinking BIG
1. D - Gutzon Borglum
2. A - Mount Rushmore is the most famous of the three mountain carvings.
3. B - All three carvings were finished by someone other than the original artist.
4. B - huge
5. A - three mountain carvings and the artist that connects them
6. D - Crazy Horse is the biggest and isn't finished yet.

The Disappearing Hair Ribbons
1. B - someone who is thought to be guilty
2. A - Pilar is upset.
3. B - Pilar's ribbons went missing before Rosa agreed to help.
4. A - Rosa searched Riley's habitat after she agreed to help.
5. A - Stinky climbed in Pilar's boot after Rosa agreed to help.
6. C - Pilar and Rosa were neighborhood detectives.

Reading: Informational

Animals of Yellowstone
1. D - He wanted to know where to look for the animals.
2. A - South Entrance and West Thumb
3. B - Elk
4. C - More animals live in forests and meadows.
5. D - an animal's home area
6. B - The wolves have the smallest population.

A Day in the City
1. D - subway
2. C - Which subway lines would you take to get to the National Archives?
3. B - They enjoy doing things together.
4. C - The White House and the National Air and Space Museum
5. A – Definition 1. - A sheet arranging information into columns or tabs
6. A - It is only on one subway line.

Family Names
1. C - to explain family names based on occupation
2. A - to move people or things
3. D - definitions and origins of occupational words
4. B - was a chef.
5. A - Fletcher and Bender
6. C - last Name

Meteor Watching
1. C - The Perseid meteor shower is a favorite.
2. A - It only happens in August.
3. C - scattered fragments of rock

4. D - The Earth takes one year to orbit the sun, and the comet takes 135 years to orbit the sun.

5. B - People enjoy watching the shower because it happens in the summer.

6. B - average

Reading: Foundational Skills

Root Words
1. cycle
2. comfort
3. bio
4. fill
5. arrange

Prefixes
1. *ir-* C: lacking responsibility
2. *anti-* B: a liquid used to keep other liquids from freezing
3. *im-* A: not able to occur
4. *mis-* D: an error
5. *pre-* B: before written records

Suffixes
1. *-ly;* A: in the right manner.
2. *-ful;* B: feeling or causing happiness
3. *-ist;* C: a person who studies science
4. *-ian;* D: a person who plays music
5. *-ment;* A: a feeling of eagerness

Writing

Nebraska Pioneer Children

1. Answers will vary.

2. Answers will vary, but should include: no electricity, food for survival, farmers were poor, so they could not afford to hire adult helpers, etc.

3. Answers will vary.

4. Boys: planting and harvesting, hunting and fishing, gathering fuel for the fire. Girls: cooking and cleaning, mending clothing, taking care of children. Answers might include physical strength, societal pressures, preparation for having a farm/husband/wife of their own one day.

The Olympics, Past and Present

1. Answers should include such elements as: Ancient were men only, they were summer only, they were conducted nude, games only included track and field type games, and they were a religious celebration. Modern are men and women, athletes wear clothing, there are MANY more events and games, they are both summer and winter.

2. Answers will vary.

3. Answers will vary.

4. Answers will vary.

Language

Language Answer Key

Prepositions
1. between
2. over
3. across
4. toward
5. around

Conjunctions
1. and - coordinating
2. because - subordinating
3. Neither/nor - correlative
4. although - subordinating
5. not only / but also - correlative
6. but - subordinating
7. and - coordinating
8. Either / or - correlative
9. unless - subordinating
10. Both / and - correlative

Verb Tenses
1. will go - C
2. cooks - A
3. rained - B
4. will visit - C
5. lives - A
6. rode
7. enjoys
8. will read
9. wanted
10. will play

Capitalization
1. Yes
2. Yes
3. No
4. Yes
5. Yes
6. No
7. Yes
8. Yes

Ending Punctuation
1. Question mark (?)
2. Period (.)
3. Period (.)
4. Exclamation point (!)
5. Question mark (?)
6. Exclamation point (!)
7. Question mark (?)
8. Period (.)
9. Question mark (?)
10. Exclamation point (!)

Commas

1. In Houston, Texas, there is a huge rodeo in February.
2. Johnny said, "Let's go play on the swings."
3. It's going to rain today, isn't it?
4. Nate had three apples, two oranges, and a banana in his lunch box.
5. Eureka, a show on the SyFy channel, is about a town of geniuses.
6. The Revolutionary War officially ended on May 12, 1784.
7. Yes, thank you, I would love some cake.
8. Along with his friends, Evan thought he could help others.
9. Because of the lightning, we could not play outside.
10. We can vacation at the beach, or we can go to the city.
11. & 12. Answers will vary

Titles

1. <u>To Kill A Mockingbird</u> is my favorite novel.
2. The headline read, "Man Kills Seven in Subway."
3. My class went to see "An Ideal Husband," a play by Oscar Wilde.
4. <u>The Avengers</u> was the best movie this summer!
5. "What Sarah Said," by Death Cab for Cutie, is the best song ever.

Changing Sentences

1. Nate and Evan go to the Houston Zoo on Sundays.
2. Dragonflies live by the river, where I hope to see some today.
3. Evan likes the monkeys that live in the primate habitat.
4. Baboons are from African and Asia, but they mostly live in zoos now.
5. Nick watches the baby giraffe as it tries to eat leaves from a tall tree.

Homophones

1. two
2. right
3. there
4. one
5. threw
6. err
7. aisle
8. ate
9. bass
10. bare

Heteronyms

1. The Polish furniture needs <u>polish</u>. (a substance to give a shiny surface)
2. I <u>object</u> to that object. (disapprove)
3. She was too close to the window to <u>close</u> it. (to shut)
4. The bass drum had a <u>bass</u> painted on it. (a fish)
5. Mr. Jones is ready to <u>present</u> the present to the President. (to give formally)
6. Don't <u>desert</u> us just because we are in the desert. (to leave)

7. The <u>dove</u> dove for the food. (a bird)
8. Give me a minute and I'll show you <u>minute</u> particles in my microscope. (tiny)
9. The singer is here to <u>record</u> a new record. (to preserve in sound)
10. I <u>refuse</u> to take out the refuse. (to say no)

Greek / Latin
1.   A. photogenic
       B. photograph
       C. telephoto
       D. photosynthesis

2.   A. aerodynamics
       B. aerobics
       C. aerate
       D. aeronautics

3.   A. epidemic
       B. democracy
       C. demographic
       D. endemic

Context Clues
1. A - moved
2. B - get rid of
3. D - denied
4. A - huge
5. C - calm

Reference Materials
1. B - (2) /ˈmin(ē)əCHər/
2. C - (3)adj. of a much smaller size than normal
       noun. a thing that is much smaller than normal
       verb. represent on a smaller scale

3. D - (4)synonyms: diminutive, tiny, small
4. A - (1) Min-i-a-ture
5. D - Encyclopedia
6. A - Dictionary
7. C - Thesaurus
8. B - Glossary

Figurative language
1. A - simile
2. D - onomatopoeia
3. E - idiom
4. B - metaphor
5. C - alliteration

Synonyms
1. big
2. hard
3. bucket
4. mad
5. talk

Antonyms
6. city
7. full
8. beautiful / pretty
9. thaw
10. catch

Practice Test Answers

Practice Test #1

Answers and Explanations

1. Part A: D: The main objective of these paragraphs is to describe Manolo's and Barry's neighborhood.

Part B: There are several sentences that can be used here. Any one that describes their neighborhood is acceptable. For example, "There are no cypresses or any other kinds of trees in Cypress Heights."

2. A: The strange thing about the name of Barry's and Manolo's neighborhood is that there are no Cypress trees and the land is flat.

3. A: The first sentence shows that Cypress Heights residents do everything in their control (painting their houses and decorating their lawns) to make their places look nice.

4. A: Barry and Manolo like living close to each other because it makes it convenient for them to visit each other.

5. C: Plants that can live in very dry climates are called drought-resistant.

6. D: Mrs. Juarez put gravel on her lawn instead of grass. She used gravel because she wouldn't have to water it.

7. B: Traditionally, new neighbors receive gifts, not give them. That is why Barry asked Mrs. Juarez that question.

8. A: Knit in this case means to join together tightly.

9. B: Thomas wanted to replace a doll he bought for his sister, which broke before the warranty was up.

10. A: The warranty or guarantee for the doll was for one year.

11. C: The word "defective" is another way of saying "broken."

12. D: The company agreed to send Thomas a replacement doll after he sent in some paperwork.

13. B: Romco asked Thomas to fill out a form and send it to them.

14. III & V: Remember that facts can be proven, but someone's opinion is debatable. Both of these statements can be debated.

15. D: The correct form for writing the name of a town and state is Anywhere, Texas.

16. A: Romco did not have time to write an individual letter to all of the customers with complaints, so they wrote a general letter to all people who complained.

17. D: It took nine days for Romco to reply to Thomas's letter according to the dates on the letters.

18. B: The tone in both letters is polite.

19. B: Hobie chose baseball because his brother was already running track and he didn't want to be compared to him.

20. A: Twinge also means to hurt. Hobie flexed his leg so fast that it made his knee hurt a little.

21. D: Always being the first one to cross the finish line is a good indication that Hobie was (and still is) a good runner.

22. A: While Martin and Hobie may be different in many ways, they are both good at running.

23. C: Hobie had a hard decision to make. Forced to give up baseball, he had to choose between playing a sport where he might be compared to his brother or staying at home. Hobie found out that difficult decisions sometimes turn out all right in the end.

24. D: The author's step-by-step account of how Hobie made it from third to first place in the race increased the tension or suspense in the story.

25. A good summary of this story would be:

"Despite showing a talent for running, Hobie chose to play baseball to avoid comparisons to his older brother. His father's accident forced him to join track, where he did well."

26. C: Hobie's breathing became ragged because he was worn out from running so fast for so long.

27. C: Hobie is most likely to rejoin track the following year as a long-distance runner, an area where he showed talent. It will also allow him to avoid comparisons to his brother, who is a sprinter.

28. Part A: B: In the story it says, "While the crack of the starting gun was still ringing in his ears," which lets you know that it was the sound of the gun.

Part B: Knowing that is was the sound of the gun the only answer that makes sense is "snap".

29. C: The author started the story with the phrase "News flash" to attract the readers' attention. The article is about a scientific fact. It is not a breaking news story.

30. B: Cohesion is a kind of stickiness in which molecules stick to each other via attraction, much in the same way a magnet sticks to metal.

31. D: The point of the experiment is to see how many pennies it takes for an already full glass of water to overflow. That is why the glass must be in a clean, dry place.

32. A: Water is sticky because its molecules stick to each other.

33. C: A paper clip can float on top of water because the molecules are stuck together and can hold it up.

34. A: The three states of water are solid, liquid, and gas.

35. C: 186.4°F is the boiling point of water at 14,000 feet.

36. D: These sentences are both facts and can be proven.

37. C: In the article it states, "Here is another fun fact about water. When it is in its solid form, ice, it is less dense."

38. A: Both articles note that water is a unique substance.

39. B: The first article talks about a property of water (its stickiness) and the second article talks about a problem related to water (pollution).

40. D: Articles about the properties of water are most likely to be found in a science text.

Practice Test #2

Answers and Explanations

1. B: The expression "rain came down in sheets" means it was raining so hard that the rain looked like it was coming down in one solid sheet rather than separate drops.

2. D: Mona and Yuri's mother was asleep after having worked overnight as a nurse.

3. C: Mona and Yuri's mother goes to bed around 7 a.m. after working all night. She usually gets up after eight hours of sleep, which would be around 3 p.m.

4. A: War is a card game. It can be played with an ordinary deck of playing cards.

5. A: When a regular deck of playing cards is used, an ace has the highest value in War and beats all other cards.

6. B: To have a "war" in the card game War, both players have to have the same card.

7. C: Mona won the first game that she and Yuri played. That is why Yuri said, "Beginner's luck."

8. A: When she said, "Actually, this game is all luck," Mona meant that the game did not require any skill to win. It just depended on the cards the players had.

9. A: Mona wins the round. A king is the second highest card in the deck. A jack is the fourth highest.

10. C: Gov. Richards taught social studies and history before getting into politics.

11. Part A: D: Paragraph 3 is mostly about Gov. Richards's achievements as governor of Texas.

Part B: A: This is the only answer choice that states one of her achievements from paragraph 3.

12. B: The word "styled" refers to how her hair was fixed.

13. A: Gov. Richards was joking about how stiff her hair was because of all the hairspray in it.

14. Part A: C: Sen. Hutchinson earned a law degree from the University of Texas in 1967.

Part B: D: The second sentence in paragraph 1 reads, "She went to the University of Texas and graduated with a law degree in 1967."

15. B: Sen. Hutchinson worked as a TV news reporter before going into politics.

16. Part A: D: Paragraph 3 is mostly about Sen. Hutchinson's accomplishments while serving as a senator.

Part B: There are several examples that could be used here. Two of them are, "She worked to fix laws that changed the way money was spent for the military. She also wrote and helped pass a law that regulated shipping on the oceans."

17. A: The abbreviation Sen. means Senator.

18. B: Gov. Richards and Sen. Hutchinson were the first women to be governor and a U.S. senator in Texas.

19. C: Both women served as the Texas State Treasurer before getting more important positions in government.

20. B: Sen. Hutchinson is still working as a U.S. Senator. Gov. Richards died in 2006, and the passage states that she left politics.

21. A: The author wrote these articles to show that women can have the same opportunities as men in Texas.

22. B: Sam called Pavarti to get directions to Pavarti's house. Sam will give the directions to her mother when they drive over the next day.

23. A: Pavarti asked Sam where she lived so that she could give Sam directions from her own house.

24. D: Sam's mother will need to turn onto Elm Street after Townline Road.

25. A: Pavarti told Sam the color of her house and the houses around it because her address is hard to see from the road.

26. A: Sam's mother should go straight on Rio Turnpike before taking a right on Main Street.

27. C: Pavarti said to, "Look for either a red truck or a small black car."

28. B: Sam is hoping that her and her mother don't get lost and have to drive up and down Main Street, especially since it runs only one way.

29. D: Sam's notes written out would look like the following: *At the third traffic light you will turn left onto Rio Turnpike. Go about half a mile until you see a 7-Eleven on the right. The next street after the 7-Eleven is Main Street.*

30. D: After buying the pumpkins, Pavarti's family is planning to have lunch before starting to carve them.

31. Part A: C: Pedro noticed the model of the 1969 Mustang because his father had talked about that type of car.

Part B: B: In the story Pedro says that his grandfather had owned a real 1969 Mustang.

32. A: Simon wanted to buy a model of a C17 fighter plane, but he didn't have enough money.

33. B: Altogether, with tax, Simon had to pay $27.

34. C: After buying Simon's model, the B17G Flying Fortress, they planned to build it and then go buy the 1969 Mustang that Pedro wanted and build that one as well.

35. D: Simon turned down his father's offer of help, but accepted Pedro's.

36. Part A: B: It is likely that Simon will invite Pedro over to help the next time he builds a model airplane.

Part B: A: This is the sentence where he says that he will probably invite Pedro over to help.

37. D: The passage gives a strong indication that Simon and Pedro are friends.

38. A: Simon lets his father drive him and Pedro to the store to buy Pedro's model of a 1969 Mustang.

39. D: Simon learned from his father that he understands that Simon is growing up and relying less on his parents and more on his friends for help.

40. C: Simon accepts a drive from his father because traffic is heavier in the afternoon than it is in the morning.

Additional Bonus Material

Due to our efforts to try to keep this book to a manageable length, we've created a link that will give you access to all of your additional bonus material.

Please visit http://www.mometrix.com/bonus948/fsag5elawb to access the information.